CHINESE COOKBOOK

Classic, Delicious & Healthy Chinese Recipes to Make at Home

(Tasting Chinese Cuisine Right in Your Little Kitchen)

Timothy Smith

Published by Sharon Lohan

© **Timothy Smith**

All Rights Reserved

Chinese Cookbook: Classic, Delicious & Healthy Chinese Recipes to Make at Home (Tasting Chinese Cuisine Right in Your Little Kitchen)

ISBN 978-1-990334-27-6

All rights reserved. No part of this guide may be reproduced in any form without permission in writing from the publisher except in the case of brief quotations embodied in critical articles or reviews.

Legal & Disclaimer

The information contained in this book is not designed to replace or take the place of any form of medicine or professional medical advice. The information in this book has been provided for educational and entertainment purposes only.

The information contained in this book has been compiled from sources deemed reliable, and it is accurate to the best of the Author's knowledge; however, the Author cannot guarantee its accuracy and validity and cannot be held liable for any errors or omissions. Changes are periodically made to this book. You must consult your doctor or get professional medical advice before using any of the suggested remedies, techniques, or information in this book.

Table of contents

Part 1 1
Introduction: Chinese Recipes: Easy and Delicious Dishes to Prepare 2
Chapter 1: About Chinese Food and Cooking 4
Chapter 2: Types of Chinese Recipes 7
Chapter 3: The Basics of Chinese Recipes and Cooking Traditions 9
Chapter 4: Basic of Chinese Cuisine 12
Chapter 5: Low Calorie Chinese Foods 15
Chapter 6: Top Ten Chinese Recipes 19
Chapter 7: Healthy Chinese Recipes 23
Chinese Spareribs 23
Noodles With Spring Onion Flavored Oil 25
Chicken Wing in SWISS Sauce 27
West Lake Fish In Vinegar Sauce 29
Wonton in Sichuan Style 32
Shanghai Pepper Steak 34
Split Pea Pudding 37
Part 2 39
01. Asian Beef with Snow Peas 40
02. Asian Beef with Snow Peas Recipe 42
03. Asian Fire Meat 44
04. Asian Fire Meat Recipe 46
05. Beef and Broccoli Recipe 48
06. Beef and Riced Broccoli Bowl 50

07. Beef Chinese Dumplings 52
08. Beef Lo Mein 54
09. Beef Lo Mein Recipe 56
10. Beef mince chow mein 58
11. Beef Stir-Fry Recipe 60
12. Beef with Vegetables 62
13. Beef with Vegetables Recipe 64
14. Beefy Chinese Dumplings 66
15. Bitter Melon and Black Bean Sauce Beef 68
16. Black Pepper Beef and Cabbage Stir Fry 70
17. Chicken and Chinese Vegetable Stir-Fry 72
18. Chicken Broccoli Ca - Unieng's Style 74
19. Chinese Barbeque Pork (Char Siu) 76
20. Chinese Beef and Broccoli Recip 79
21. Chinese Beef With Broccoli 81
22. Chinese Chicken Fried Rice 83
23. Chinese Ginger & Horseradish Beef 85
24. Chinese Noodle Chicken Recipe 87
25. Chinese Pepper Steak Recipe 89
26. Chinese Pork Tenderloin 91
27. Chinese Roast Pork 93
28. Chinese Spareribs Recipe 95
29. Crispy Ginger Beef 97
30. Crispy Orange Beef 99
31. Crispy Orange Beef Recipes 101
32. Eggplant with Garlic Sauce 103
33. Flavorful Beef Stir-Fry 105

34. General Tso's Chicken Recipe 107
35. Grilled Asian Chicken Recipe 109
36. Grilled Hoisin Beef Recipe 111
37. Honey Walnut Shrimp Recipe 113
38. Hot and Tangy Broccoli Beef 115
39. Kikkoman Chinese Pepper Steak 117
40. Kung Pao Chicken Recipe 119
41. Ma Po Tofu Recipe 121
42. Minchee (Chinese Beef & Potato Hash) 123
43. Mongolian Beef 125
44. Mongolian Beef and Spring Onions 127
45. Mongolian Beef I Recipe 129
46. Mongolian Beef II 131
47. Moo Goo Gai Pan Recipe 133
48. Orange Peel Beef Recipe 135
49. Peking Duck Recipe 137
50. Peking Pork Chops Recipe 139
51. Potstickers (Chinese Dumplings) 140
52. Restaurant Style Beef and Broccoli 142
53. Shrimp with Lobster Sauce 144
54. Slow Cooker Mongolian Beef 146
55. Spicy Beef Filet in Oyster Sauce 148
56. Spicy Crispy Beef Recipe 150
57. Spicy Orange Zest Beef 152
58. Steamed Fish with Ginger 154
59. Stir-Fried Chicken With Pineapple and Peppers 156
60. Stir-Fry Pork with Ginger 158

61. Super-Spicy Mongolian Beef 159
62. Super-Spicy Mongolian Beef Recipe 161
63. Sweet and Sour Chicken I 162
64. Sweet and Sour Pork III 164
65. Sweet and Sour Pork Tenderloin Recipe 167
66. Szechuan Beef Recipe 169
67. Szechuan Spicy Eggplant 171
68. Szechwan Shrimp Recipe 173
69. Ten Minute Szechuan Chicken Recipe 175
70. Tsao's Chicken II 177
Pepper Steak With Mushrooms 180
Sesame Beef Stir fry 182
Beef And Snow Pea Stir-Fry 184
Ginger Beef 185
Beef with Broccoli 186
Spicy Beef Stir Fry 187

Part 1

Introduction: Chinese Recipes: Easy and Delicious Dishes to Prepare

Chinese people consider their cooking as a workmanship rather than an art like the vast majority. They trust that their food symbolizes a feeling of social associations. The ordinary convention of cooking Chinese food is made with loads of grains, vegetables, meats and different starches. The Chinese people feel that eating Chinese food implies that the stomach must be content all together to everything else to be content

Chinese people have taken it upon themselves to approach food with deference. Numerous people who experience Chinese food, can comprehend the Chinese society and their affection for life taking into account the way they cook. They generally say that you can comprehend and gain from another society and their lifestyles through their cooking. In the same way as other societies, the Chinese express their adoration for life and profound being through their different foods and respectable neighborliness.

The Chinese dependably make others feel like they are at home through their greetings, cooking and infectious warm invites. It is a delight to realize that Chinese people express bunches of adoration through their cooking and society.

In a Chinese home knowing your social graces is an absolute necessity. These behaviors show regard for the elderly and more for more astute grown-ups. It is a piece of their way of life and convictions. Another piece of their way of life is to set up the food and present it in a guileful way. They make the most of their cooking for others, as well as they have a great time doing as such.

The Chinese are well disposed regarding the matter of meeting and welcome people. They want to make others feel at home and a piece of their family too. Chinese food has turned into one of numerous acclaimed social foods that everybody cherishes and appreciates far and wide. It demonstrates that the Chinese people have gratefulness for their food and are appreciative to have visitors who make the most of their cooking.

Chapter 1: About Chinese Food and Cooking

Chinese quality recipes are simple and delicious, making them a fantastic option for individuals nights once your family is in a big hurry but still would like to get a warm, tasty meal. You simply need quick and easy tools to begin creating China tasty recipes in your house, together with your favorite diner specialties.

All that you should make basic Asian recipes is a wok as well as a bamboo steamer. Made specifically for use with a wok, though you may also want to invest in a small slotted wok spoon, which is almost like a spatula. You can even need to have a very well-defined knife, or perhaps a cleaver, available. Numerous simple China quality recipes demand finely diced vegetables and meats, building a sharp knife a necessary instrument for Asian food preparation.

Oriental dishes frequently involve utilizing a bamboo steamer, which can be acquired cheaply within a local shop or bought on the internet. There are several tips that will help you create your China food healthy and delicious utilizing your steamer, that ought to be applied more than a wok or big pot of cooking water.

First, you will want to make sure that the water you are using is boiling, and producing steam before you add the food to the steamer. This may keep the meals flavorful and fresh, rather than humid and deteriorating.

You need to be sure that you have enough water in your wok to cook the plate without the need of including far more h2o, in order that the water is creating heavy steam throughout the food preparation time for the recipe. Chinese cooking will become easier with practice, but until you are an expert, you will have to experiment a little.

You might also are interested to buy some fundamental China components, such as soy sauce, oyster sauce, sesame gas, cornflour and ginger. Getting the essentials readily available will allow you to easily prepare food your best Oriental dishes without needing to come up with a special journey to the supermarket to get items.

You can always review your favorite recipes before your next trip to the supermarket, and pick the items that you will need later for cooking them. Some items, for example ginger herb, helps keep for many years providing you keep it refrigerated, while other items ought to always be new.

After you have expended a little while testing Asian you, cooking and your loved ones will know which Oriental quality recipes you enjoy finest, in order to maintain stocks of the constituents you will need with significantly less speculating.

You will discover a number of tasty recipes using an on-line search engine, which will also let you for more information on Oriental food and the ways to prepare them. Many of the most well-known recipes are easy to discover on the web, such as Kung Pao fowl, Oriental steamed sea food, fried rice or wonderful and bad pork. Discovering several Chinese tasty recipes on-line will likely let you prepare your pantry and tools for producing your chosen China food items in your house. Numerous web sites are able to offer a thorough list of the things you have to get started out.

Chapter 2: Types of Chinese Recipes

Once you go to China recipes, there are different kinds of recipes. Everybody has their preferred food but all dining places may not be utilizing the same quality recipes for doing it.

When you attempt to really make it one thing will result in you a lot of troubles as a result you could have to use often times to get it the way you want it to be. If you want to get the best recipes then you have to spend some extra money for a cookbook which is being hand down through family lines.

Asian tasty recipes standard sorts are seafood, meats, rice, noodles and vegetable. These dishes could be from various areas of the chinese suppliers for instance your Lo Mein don't flavor that great since it does from the Shanghai.

In chinese suppliers food is important a good deal as well as every region than it features its own recipes and taste. Excellent dining places integrate together with the various locations in asia in order to provide the actual flavor from the foods where it is well-known.

As folks the North section of the asia use wheat and noodlesnoodles and people in the southern part of area use rice and rice flour with their dishes. As the far east is really a big country consequently it provides distinct environment in northern as well as in southern that also impact the recipes.

Asian recipes use several types of dishes which will make them truly tasty and more pleasing. The most famous Chinese hot and spicy plate is Kung Pao. Generally combined with shrimp or poultry and it also is comprised of pepper marinade so we can adjust the degree of heat as we should.

All Asian recipes have one thing in frequent are often the noodles, meat and ricevegetable and meat in them excluding the area or hot and spicy component from it. There are many exceptions like pancakes and soups which are actually renowned Chinese meals and therefore are great quality recipes that one need.

Chapter 3: The Basics of Chinese Recipes and Cooking Traditions

Chinese cookery traditions are usually identified for presenting the ideal amalgamation of taste, presentation and aroma. Cooking food various Chinese food items is recognized as equally as one particular art in the united states. Some of the surprising things of Oriental recipes is fragrance, Color and aroma. Multicolored materials starting with light-weight environmentally friendly to darkish white and greenwhite, yellow, caramel, black and red colour are mainly applied. Creative show is an important element to Chinese foods. This item goes through the diverse local cooking food different types of Asia. You may also locate some real Asian food products right here.

China Foods Variations and Benefits:
Nourishment is also specific ideal well worth in several facets of China cooking. Usage of remedial plants and flowers such as new ginger underlying, scallions, dried out lily buds, tree and garlic fungi is regular. Chinese cooking tradition offers a notion depending on which

food and medicines are mostly belongs to similar source.

With its fat-free food and low-calorie, it is tiny delight that China meals is indeed approved around the world. Oriental food items meals usually do not carry several sweet meals. A primary reason is the Oriental generally tend to finish their night time dinner by using a fresh fruit contrary to Westerners who prefer a deserts. One more cause is that ice-cold sweet dishes never found place in Chinese cuisine due to insufficient a refrigerator in several homes. Many of the Chinese fairly sweet meals are specially prepared and functioned on certain circumstances like Moon and functions events.

Extremely the majority of the principle China recipes are favored to get consumed utilizing the Chopsticks. Therefore if you happen to be planning to drop by China, you'd do well to go to a neighborhood Chinese restaurant and attempt using chopsticks. The concept of chopsticks is attached to the experience of Confucius. The make use of of knife and fork was thought to be brutal and also the chopsticks symbolized benevolence and gentleness.

The Cookery Types of Preparing food Chinese Dishes:
You will find majorly half a dozen localised preparing food kinds implemented in The far east, i.e Shanghai, Hunan, Mandarin, Szechwan and Hakka and Cantonese. Crispy fried noodles with vegetables and

Beef, Shark Fin soups, Sugary and bitter pork and Deep fried crispy fowl are acknowledged Cantonese Chinese food foods. Cantonese food preparation entails mix frying, deeply frying and steaming to bring out the top rated taste with the substances.

Mild and uncomplicated sauces are the fact of Cantonese food preparation. Usage of garlic clove, early spring red onion,salt and sugar, soy products marinade, rice vino, corn starchy foods and essential oil is crucial for many food.

Chapter 4: Basic of Chinese Cuisine

Asia is a substantial nation with numerous regions, each using their personal distinct style and tastes of food: Anhui (Hui), Cantonese (Yue), Fujian (Min), Hunan (Xiang), Jiangsu (Su or Yang), Shandong (Lu), Szechuan (Chuan) and Zhejiang (Zhe). Additionally, emigrants from Asia can be obtained around the world, and those emigrants have formulated equally new variations on standard China recipes, by adapting Chinese meals to nearby choices, and entirely new food.

Most Oriental food made up of two primary components:

1. Zhush? which in Mandarin indicates "major foods" - Rice, noodles or steamed buns ("mantou").
2. C? i which in Mandarin implies "veggie" - Several associated dishes of meats, sea food or fresh vegetables.

Some preferred Oriental meals involve:
- Dumplings - Dumplings made up of soil (minced) meats and/or veggies. They might be boiled ("shuijiao"), fried ("guotie") or steamed ("jiaozi").

- Xiaolongbao - Steamed buns containing beef soups (various meats gelatin is put within the bun prior to steaming, the steam temperature melts the gelatin into soups), sea food or vegetables. Xiaolongbao made out of elevated flour are normal throughout Asia and therefore are referred to as "baozi". Inside the Southern of the country, xiaolongbao may also be at times produced employing unraised flour.

Sometimes cornmeal, millet, barley or sorghum are used, though - Congee - A porridge, usually made from rice.
- Soy ovum - A difficult-boiled egg cell in soy products water, sugar and sauce, flavoured with herbs and spices.
- Kung Pao (or Kung Po) chicken breast - A spicy chicken recipe flavored with Sichuan peppercorns, Shaoxing wine, and unroasted cashew peanuts or nuts. Westernized versions using in your area readily available China ingredients and bell peppers are well-liked from the United Europe and States.
- General Tso's chicken - A sweet and spicy deep-fried chicken dish that is popular in Chinese restaurants in the United Canada and States, but is practically unknown in China itself.

- Peking duck - The trademark plate of Beijing: A duck, glazed by using a syrup and then roasted. The plate is traditionally carved looking at diners and ingested with scallions, plum marinade and steamed pancakes (Mandarin: pinyin). In britain, the meal is normally referred to as "crispy aromatic duck" and is also prepared employing aromatic seasoning such as 5-liven powder, and by frying the duck as opposed to roasting.
- Zongzi - Glutinous rice with assorted tooth fillings, covered with bamboo foliage after which boiled or steamed.

Chapter 5: Low Calorie Chinese Foods

According to the statistics, there are more Chinese restaurants in the country than any other type of ethnic restaurant combined. If you think about it for a couple of minutes, you can probably name at least a handful of Chinese restaurants in your area right off the top of your head, although this is an astonishing fact, when you think about all the pizza joints and Mexican restaurants that are around. Doing so can be detrimental to your health, even though everyone loves to eat exotic dishes of fried rice, Szechuan Beef, and sweet and sour pork from their local favorite. You can learn to cook low calorie Chinese recipes in your own home, by learning a few basic tips.

Initial, let's examine why ingesting at or acquiring takeout from the favored consuming spot is not really a good choice for you typically. The food is extremely oily. That is one of the things that you will notice when eating at most Asian restaurants. Simply because strong frying takes on a central part in the planning of numerous food. Have you ever wondered why the beef in your favorite Asian having spot is usually far more sensitive and succulent than once you try to recreate dishes in your own home? It's because these facilities make use of a method referred to as essential oil blanching. Oil blanching is a procedure wherein the meats of your choosing (seafood, chicken and beef and so forth.) is marinated in a combination of seasonings and cornstarch and after that serious fried at a low heat. The hot oil seals in the juices into the meat and also causes the cornstarch on the surface of the meat to gelatinize, leaving the cook with a piece of juicy, tender meat,. That's what happens during this process. Even if this cooking food approach brings flavorful meat, furthermore, it renders fundamentally low calorie food products into fatty bombs. Oils includes about 120 unhealthy calories for every tablespoon and whenever you serious fry, particularly on the low conditions necessary for oil blanching, the meals that you will be frying has a tendency to process a copious amount, leading you to consume a huge selection of unneeded energy.

Together with gas blanching, a great deal of meals depend on traditional deep frying to find the desired composition and final results that the make would like. As an example, popular dishes like fairly sweet and bitter pork or Szechuan beef are usually filled with gas through the deeply excess fat fryer. Even recipes like fried rice and stir fried fresh vegetables may become fatty, fattening meals in the hands of an unskilled chef.

Fortunately, there are a few tips and tricks that you can use at home in order to slash the calories from your favorite Asian dishes. Not only will you help your waistline, but you will also help your bottom line since cooking at home is much more economical than getting takeout. You can duplicate the results by using a water blanching technique, a process which is very similar to blanching vegetables, if you want to have succulent and tender meat like you would get from the oil blanching technique. Very first, you will have to marinate your lean meats in a combination of egg whites, sodium, and cornstarch. Then, provide a container of water for the boil. Add the meat into the pot and cook for about thirty seconds. Alternatively, just until the raw color of the meat has disappeared. Afterward, get rid of the various meats in the pot and give it time to drain properly. Following that, you are able to carry on with the beloved China stir fry menu.

Yet another hint which you can use would be to prepare with non-adhere pots and pans. A low-put area will allow you to prepare food China meals in the home without having to use plenty of gas to stop adhering. Rather than making use of tablespoons of organic gas to lubricate your pan, that can include numerous calorie consumption to the Chinese meals, use a couple of aerosols of cooking mist, which happens to be below 15.

Eventually, replacement some of the meats within your plate with greens to make a low calorie China formula. Meat contains far more calories, fat, and cholesterol than vegetables, so by substituting some of the protein with additional vegetables, you can help to slash your caloric intake by weight. Think of using veggies as the centerpiece of your Asian recipe and also the various meats among your seasoning elements.

You can cook low calorie Chinese recipes in the comfort of your own home, by knowing a couple of easy tricks. As you control the standard of the constituents and the cooking food strategies, your final plate will probably be much healthier and less expensive than nearly anything you can order in your beloved Asian eatery.

Chapter 6: Top Ten Chinese Recipes

If you love to use simple, fresh ingredients with short cooking time, chinese food is a delicious way to expand your personal recipe book, particularly. These top 10 recipes are well-known around the world, and are should-haves within your variety of Oriental tasty recipes.

Fried rice is the ultimate Chinese food, and can be one of the most flexible in your cookbook because you can use leftover ingredients and rice to make it, fried Rice - A popular item in Chinese restaurants. Needless to say, you can utilize refreshing elements but it's recommended to make use of rice that has been stored in the refrigerator over night for optimum effects. Components usually involved with generating fried rice are eggs, spring red onion, diced meats of sometimes beef, chicken or pork, ham, prawns and vegetables for example bean carrots, celery, peas, corn and sprouts. There are several forms of fried rice but the far more famous versions are definitely the Yong Chow and Fukien fried rice.

Kung Pao Chicken breast - Kung Pao chicken breast or Kung Po fowl is really a Asian dish from Szechuan food and is regarded as a delicacy. The formula with this tasty meal typically requires diced chicken that is certainly pre-marinated and easily stir-fried with saltless roasted peanuts, red bell peppers, sherry or rice vino, hoisin marinade, sesame oil, oyster marinade, and chili peppers. On the other hand, you may use shrimp, scallops, meat or pork instead of the poultry.

Moo Shu Pork - This is a meal of upper Asian origin as well as a favorite of countless. Components inside a Mushu pork dish usually entail environmentally friendlycarrots and cabbage, timber ear canal mushrooms, coffee bean sprouts, scallions, scrambled eggs and time lily buds. Bell peppers, snowfall pea pods,onions and celery, Shiitake mushrooms and bok choy are occasionally utilized. With the exception for bean sprouts and day lily buds, the vegetables are cut into thin and long strips before cooking. Fried Mushu pork is going to be covered with moo shu pancakes that is brushed with hoisin sauce and ingested yourself. Moo shu pancakes are thin wrappers made of flour that is easily available in supermarkets and steamed right before eating.

General Tso's Fowl - Basic Tso's chicken breast can be a Hunan cuisine that likes spicy and sweet and incredibly well-known in Oriental dining places in America and Canada in which it's usually marked as being a "chef's area of expertise". General Tso's Poultry menu generally requires battered fowl serious-fried and marinated withginger and garlic, rice white vinegar, soy sauce, sesame oil, Shaoxing wine or scallions, sugar and sherry and very hot chili peppers.

Spring season Rolls - Spring season moves make wonderful snacks and appetizers. Are slightly different to its cousin, even though they are similar to egg rolls. Springs rolls are have much less satisfying than ovum rolls, is small in dimensions along with its skin is finer. To produce a spring season roll, minced various meats and thinly minimize strips of fresh vegetables are rolled and sealed within a square or rounded rice papers. This will make it strong fried until crispy and golden brownish. Offer this crowd pleaser piping warm.

Chinese Dumplings - Asian dumplings can be a wonderful addition to your residence cooked foods, and can be produced simply and quickly making use of only a couple of components. The important thing to creating an outstanding dumpling is to make sure that all your elements are finely minced, to ensure that each of the dumplings are steamed from the same amount of time.

Beef and Broccoli - The real key to preparing food up a delicious Meat and Broccoli meal in your house is to make a great sauce made up of oyster marinade, light-weight soy products sauce, thicker soy products cornstarch and sauce solution. Marinade the beef just before blend frying with sweets, rice white vinegar, cornstarch option, soy products marinade and sugar.

Sweet and Sour Pork - This tasty-sugary remarkably well-liked Asian recipe is of Cantonese beginning. It is actually a good dish to put together when you are planning on possessing visitors, who will be extremely pleased with your cooking food expertise. As with other Chinese food recipes, the key to making a great Sweet and Sour Pork dish is in the sauce made ofketchup and sugar, white vinegar, and soy sauce. Its elements incorporatepineapple and pork, bell pepper and onion lower into chew dimensions parts.

Chow Mein - In American citizen Chinese dishes, Chow Mein can be a mix-fried meal consisting of noodles, meat such typically pork, shrimp, chicken and beefpork, other and cabbage vegetables.

Dice Suey - Chop suey or "za sui" or "shap sui" literally implies 'mixed pieces' is surely an American citizen-China meal typically comprised of left over meats and vegetables stir fried easily inside a sauce thickened with starch. It is a great plate when you should employ the very last of yesterday's fowl or pork roast and will include lean meats of any type for example shrimp, chicken and fish pork or meat and other vegetables from celery to coffee bean cabbage and sprouts. Dice Suey is usually ingested with rice.

Chapter 7: Healthy Chinese Recipes

Chinese Spareribs

Ingredients:

1 pound pork chop

Marinade:

1 tsp glucose

1 tbsp gentle soya marinade

1 tsp darker soya marinade

1 tsp cornstarch

1 tsp normal water

1 tsp essential oil

1 tsp Shaoxing wine (or any Chinese cooking vino)

1/2 tsp sesame essential oil and tiny pepper

Preparation:

1 always rinse and wipe dry pork cut

2 lb with the back of the chopper to tenderize
3 mixture with marinade and set up away for 30mins - 1 hr
4 temperature 2 cups of oils, reduce pork slice with moderate popular oil and fry right up until prepared

Ideas:
Remember to switch to maximum hot oil before remove from pan, this can move away the excessive oil to reduce greasy and eat healthy.

Noodles With Spring Onion Flavored Oil

Ingredients:

4 ounce Shanghai noodle (or any Chinese noodle, dry bodyweight)

6 stalks spring season-onion

1/4 glass oils

3 tbsp dark soya sauce

3 tbsp water

1.5 tsp sweets

Preparation:

1 put 1 tsp salt in a cooking pot of warm water, prepare noodles, refresh and remove with tap water, drain properly

2 always rinse and lower spring season-onion into portions

3 temperature the gas, fry early spring-onion in medium sized hot essential oil until golden brownish and crispy.

4 Arrange springtime onion, leave 2 tbsp right behind

5 add more 1 tbsp darkish soya marinade and 1 tbsp drinking water, .5 tsp sweets and mixture properly, add early spring-onion to the marinade and fry right up until nicely flavoured, eliminate

6 heating the remaining 2 tbsp dark soya sauce and two tbsp h2o, 1 tsp sugar and combine properly.

7 add more noodles and chuck uniformly, spread with 1 tbsp of springtime-onion flavour oil, and Provide.

If you found nothing from your refrigerator, just got noodles and spring oil left from your last dishes, try this recipe. No meet is essential. Your will see the initial flavor from spring-onion, an important ingredient in Asian food preparation

Chicken Wing in SWISS Sauce

Ingredients:

6 frozen chicken breast wings in complete, around 700-750g

1 thick portion ginger herb

3 stalks spring season onion

Sauce:

5 tbsp gentle soya sauce

5 tbsp darkish soya marinade

1 tbsp sesame oils

1 tbsp Shaoshing red wine (or any China wine)

2 computers rock sweets (kitchen table golf), burglary small pieces

2 servings of water

Preparation:

1 unfreeze the fowl wash, rinse and wings

2 blanch the wings in boiling water for 1 remove, put and min in chilly normal water, increase

3 heating 2 tbsp essential oil, fry the ginger cut and spring season onion for around 1 min, put thesauce and boil until finally all sugar liquefy

4 include the wings within the sauce until finally reboil

5 use light fire, protect then keep boil about 15 mins

6 convert the wings to a different one part, away from the fireplace, abandon the wings within the marinade with include for one more 10 mins.

West Lake Fish In Vinegar Sauce

Ingredients:

1 Entire Seafood - approx 2 pounds (lawn carp, snapper, water largemouth bass or any white species of fish)

6 cups drinking water

4 - 5 pieces of ginger

1 stalk scallion - well sliced

1/3 cup cider vinegar - or black color (Chiangkang) vinegar if available

1/4 cup glucose - brownish or white sugars can be used

2 tbsp soy sauce

2 tbsp rice wines

2 tbsp cornstarch

Crunch of sodium

Asian Celery (Qin Cai) - for garnishing

Preparation:

From the traditional way of making this plate, the sea food is defined within a basin water and starved for a couple of-3 days to take out any muddy taste.

Wash or always rinse the seafood. Make sure you eliminate gills, and scales. By using a distinct blade, slice 2 or 3 diagonal slashes on both sides in the seafood.

If you want to make it artistic, slice 2 - 3 diagonal cuts on one side of the fish. And then on the reverse side, you may also slit the flesh through the tail approximately the top from the sea food. Do that by carefully urgent in the sea food although cutting through the tail, and down the anchor.

In the large cooking pot, provide the 6 servings of normal water to some boil together with the scallion and ginger. Make sure to have enough drinking water to pay for the species of fish so that you don't have to transform the fish as it may split the flesh.

Poach the seafood for approximately 8 to 10 mins. Empty, and after that set-aside.

To make sauce:

Boil 1/2cup of water. The water utilized to boil the seafood can be used as a result of added taste from your ginger and scallion. Otherwise, poultry carry may be used.

Add inside the soysauce and sugar, and vinegar. Simmer over a method warmth to break down the glucose.

Mix the rice cornstarch and wine in a bowl, before pouring it in to thicken the sauce. Make sure to stir consistently to protect yourself from lumps.

Get rid of from season and heat with sodium. Black color pepper is non-obligatory.

Servicing:

Put the seafood inside a platter and put the sauce around. For garnishing, set some pieces of Chinese celery (qin cai) on the top. You may also put a dash of sesame oil or minced garlic before serving.

Wonton in Sichuan Style

Ingredients:

4 oz minced pork

16 bedding prepared-produced wonton wrapper

Spices:

1/2 tbsp egg white-colored

1/4 tsp salt

1/2 tsp gentle soya sauce

1/2 tsp China Wines

very little pepper and sesame oil

Dipping sauce (most important):

1 tsp cut early spring onion

1 tsp sliced garlic

1 tsp darkish vinegar

1/2 tsp terrain Sichuan peppercorn

2 tbsp light soya marinade

1/2 tbsp dark soya sauce

1 tsp sugars

1 tbsp chilli oil

Preparation:

1 year the minced pork to help make the satisfying

2 place 1 tsp of your satisfying on each and every wonton sheet, design into wonton

(wrapping strategy, please make reference to Generating Wonton

3 mixture the dipping sauce together and place in a tureen

4 cook the wonton in boiling water until finally carried out in close to 8-10mins. Toss nicely using the dipping marinade.

Shanghai Pepper Steak

Ingredients:

1.25 lb. meat pieces (the better tender, the more effective)

2 tbsp. canola gas

1 mug diced green bell pepper (with a lot of seeds and membrane taken out)

1 mug diced reddish bell pepper (with most seeds and membrane removed)

1 cup diced celery

1 mug diced yellowish onion

1 tbsp. corn starch

2 tsp. light brown sugar

1 14 oz. can beef broth

1/4 cup drinking water

1/2 mug soy products sauce

2 tbsp. rice white vinegar

1 tsp. sesame seeds

1 tsp. coarsely floor black pepper

1/4 tsp. white-colored pepper

1/4 tsp. crushed red pepper

1.5 glasses (free of moisture) Grandfather Ben's? Changed? rice and ingredients called

for in guidelines on box.

Preparation:

- According to the instructions on box Prepare the rice. Within a big skillet, temperature the oil.
- Add more the heat and meat, stirring typically, until finally the various meats is brownish on all sides.
- Deplete off of about one half from the water from skillet. Add more the new fruit and vegetables and continue to stir
- often, until fruit and vegetables are sensitive (but don't overcook!).
- Put the meat broth, the soy marinade and the rice vinegar and then all the dried up ingredients apart from the corn starchy foods.
- Carry on and stir typically. Combinethe cornstarch into the 1/4 glass of frosty drinking water and increase skillet,

- Consistently stir until finally gravy thickens. Provide about the rice.
- Servesabout 6.

Split Pea Pudding

Ingredients:

20 ounce yellowish break up peas

3 oz cornstarch

1 glass coconut whole milk

6 oz new milk

1/2 oz agar

4 mugs drinking water

5 oz sugars

Preparation

1. Rinse your form with chilly drinking water.

2. Simmer yellow split peas until the peas smooth. Rinse and deplete.

3. Combine cornstarch with coconut dairy and refreshing milk products.

4. Liquefy agar in 4 glasses boilingwater and drain, and mix in milk and sugar option. When thicken, put yellowish divide peas and mix it effectively.

5. Fill mixture inside your mould, chill and cool.

6. Minimize into dense pieces, wise to serve cold.

You might consider using some sorts of animated pudding moulds, sweets moulds or ice cubes generating moulds. The pudding should come out much more wonderful, and your visitor can have more enjoyable.

Part 2

01. Asian Beef with Snow Peas

Ingredients

3 tablespoons soy sauce soy sauce
2 tablespoons rice rice wine
1 tablespoon brown sugar brown sugar
1/2 teaspoon cornstarch cornstarch
1 tablespoon vegetable oil vegetable oil
1 tablespoon ginger root minced fresh ginger root
1 tablespoon garlic minced garlic
1 pound beef round steaks beef round steak cut into thin strips
8 ounces snow peas snow peas

Directions

In a little bowl, combine the soy sauce, rice wine, brown sugar and cornstarch. Reserve.

Heat oil in a wok or skillet over medium high temperature. Stir-fry ginger and garlic for 30 seconds. Add the steak and stir-fry for 2 minutes or until evenly browned. Add the snow peas and stir-fry for yet another three minutes. Add the soy sauce mixture, bring to a boil, stirring constantly. Lower heat and simmer before sauce is thick and smooth. Serve immediately.

02. Asian Beef with Snow Peas Recipe

Ingredients

3 tablespoons soy sauce
2 tablespoons rice wine
1 tablespoon brown sugar
1/2 teaspoon cornstarch
1 tablespoon vegetable oil
1 tablespoon minced fresh ginger root
1 tablespoon minced garlic
1 pound beef round steak, cut into thin strips
8 ounces snow peas

Directions

In a little bowl, combine the soy sauce, rice wine, brown sugar and cornstarch. Reserve.

Heat oil in a wok or skillet over medium high temperature. Stir-fry ginger and garlic for 30 seconds. Add the steak and stir-fry for 2 minutes or until evenly browned. Add the snow peas and stir-fry for yet another three minutes. Add the soy sauce mixture, bring to a boil, stirring constantly. Lower heat and simmer before sauce is thick and smooth. Serve immediately.

03. Asian Fire Meat

Ingredients

1/2 cup soy sauce soy sauce
1 tablespoon sesame oil sesame oil
2 tablespoons brown sugar brown sugar
3 cloves garlic garlic crushed
1 red onion large red onion chopped
black pepper ground black pepper to taste
1 teaspoon red pepper flakes red pepper flakes
2 tablespoons sesame seeds sesame seeds
2 leeks leeks leeks chopped
1 carrot small carrot chopped
1 pound beef round steaks beef round steak sliced paper thin

Directions

Step 1 1 In a big bowl, mix together the soy sauce, sesame oil, brown sugar, garlic, and red onion. Stir in the black pepper, red pepper flakes, sesame seeds, leeks and carrot. Mix in the meat yourself to make sure even coating. Cover and let marinate for at least 2 hours or overnight.

Step 2 2 Brush underneath half a wok with cooking oil, and heat over medium-high heat. Devote each of the meat and marinade simultaneously, and cook stirring constantly. The meat will be cooked after only a few minutes. Remove from heat and serve with rice or noodles. For Korean-style fire meat, roll the meat mixture up in a leaf of red lettuce.

04. Asian Fire Meat Recipe

Ingredients

1/2 cup soy sauce
1 tablespoon sesame oil
2 tablespoons brown sugar
3 cloves garlic, crushed
1 large red onion, chopped
ground black pepper to taste
1 teaspoon red pepper flakes
2 tablespoons sesame seeds
2 leeks leeks, chopped
1 small carrot, chopped
1 pound beef round steak, sliced paper thin

Directions

Step 1 1 In a big bowl, mix together the soy sauce, sesame oil, brown sugar, garlic, and red onion. Stir in the black pepper, red pepper flakes, sesame seeds, leeks and carrot. Mix in the meat yourself to make sure even coating. Cover and let marinate for at least 2 hours or overnight.

Step 2 2 Brush underneath half a wok with cooking oil, and heat over medium-high heat. Devote each of the meat and marinade simultaneously, and cook stirring constantly. The meat will be cooked after a few minutes. Remove from heat and serve with rice or noodles. For Korean-style fire meat, roll the meat mixture up in a leaf of red lettuce.

05. Beef and Broccoli Recipe

Ingredients

1/2 cup oyster sauces
1 tablespoon asian (toasted) sesame oil
1/2 cup sherry
1 1/2 teaspoons soy sauce
1 1/2 teaspoons white sugar
1 1/2 teaspoons cornstarch
1 pound beef round steak, cut into 1/8-inch thick strips
4 1/2 tablespoons vegetable oil, plus more if needed
1 1/2 thin slice of fresh ginger root
1 1/2 tablespoons garlic, peeled and smashed
1 1/2 pounds broccoli, cut into florets

Directions

Step one 1 Whisk together the oyster sauce, sesame oil, sherry, soy sauce, sugar, and cornstarch in a bowl, and stir before sugar has dissolved. Place the steak pieces right into a shallow bowl, pour the oyster sauce mixture over the meat, stir to coat well, and marinate for at least thirty minutes in refrigerator.

Step two 2 Heat vegetable oil in a wok or large skillet over medium-high heat, and stir in the ginger and garlic. Let them sizzle in the hot oil for approximately 1 minute to flavor the oil, then remove and discard. Stir in the broccoli, and toss and stir in the hot oil until bright green and almost tender, 5 to 7 minutes. Take away the broccoli from the wok, and reserve.

Step 3 3 Pour a bit more oil in to the wok, if needed, and stir and toss the beef with the marinade before sauce forms a glaze on the beef, and the meat is no more pink, about five minutes. Return the cooked broccoli to the wok, and stir before meat and broccoli are heated through, about three minutes.

06. Beef and Riced Broccoli Bowl

Ingredients

1/2 cup beef broth
1/4 cup hoisin sauce
2 tablespoons reduced-sodium soy sauce
2 tablespoons sesame oils, divided
1 tablespoon oyster sauces
1 tablespoon cornstarch
1 teaspoon brown sugar
1 1/4 pounds new york strip steak, thinly sliced into bite-sized pieces
2 tablespoons butter
2 (10-ounce) bags frozen broccoli rice
1 teaspoon minced garlic
1 teaspoon salt
1/2 teaspoon ground black pepper
1 teaspoon toasted sesame seeds, or to taste
teaspoon ? red pepper flakes, or to taste

Directions

Step one 1 Whisk together beef broth, hoisin sauce, soy sauce, 1 tablespoon sesame oil, oyster sauce, cornstarch, and brown sugar in a bowl until cornstarch and sugar are dissolved.

Step two 2 Place sliced steak in another bowl and drizzle with remaining 1 tablespoon of sesame oil. Stir until evenly coated.

Step three 3 Melt butter in a big skillet over medium-high heat. Add broccoli rice, garlic, salt, and pepper. Cook for five minutes; stirring occasionally. Divide broccoli rice into serving bowls.

Step 4 Add beef to the skillet. Cook over medium-high heat, stirring continually, for five minutes. Pour sauce over beef and cook for 5 more minutes or until sauce has thickened.

Step 5 Spoon beef over broccoli rice. Garnish with sesame seeds and crushed red pepper.

07. Beef Chinese Dumplings

Ingredients

1 1/5 lbs ground beef
1 2/3 cups shredded chinese cabbage
4/5 carrot, shredded
4/5 onion, minced
4/5 egg
13/16 teaspoon sugar
13/16 teaspoon salt
2 3/8 teaspoons soy sauce
2 3/8 teaspoons vegetable oil
2/3 pound package wonton wrappers

Directions

In a big bowl, mix together beef, cabbage, carrot, and onion. Stir in the egg, sugar, salt, soy sauce, and vegetable oil.

Place a big teaspoonful of filling in the guts of a dumpling skin. Moisten the edges of a wonton with a few drops of water. Then fold the dumpling in two, and pinch the edges together to seal. Create a ripple pattern along the pinched edge by pinching and gently pushing together small segments of it. Repeat with remaining dumplings.

Boil the dumplings in water until they float to the most notable, about 5 minutes.

08. Beef Lo Mein

Ingredients

1 1/2 (8-ounce) packages spaghetti
1 1/2 teaspoons dark sesame oil
1 1/2 tablespoons peanut oil
6 tablespoons garlic, minced
1 1/2 tablespoons minced fresh ginger root
6 cups mixed vegetables
1 1/2 pounds flank steak, thinly sliced
4 1/2 tablespoons reduced-sodium soy sauce
3 tablespoons brown sugar
1 1/2 tablespoons oyster sauces
1 1/2 tablespoons asian chile paste with garlic

Directions

Step 1 1 Bring a big pot of lightly salted water to a boil. Cook spaghetti in the boiling water until cooked through but firm to the bite, about 12 minutes; drain and transfer to a big bowl. Drizzle sesame oil over the spaghetti; toss to coat. Place a plate atop the bowl to keep carefully the noodles warm.

Step two 2 Heat peanut oil in a wok or large skillet over medium-high heat. Cook and stir garlic and ginger in hot oil until fragrant, about 30 seconds. Add mixed vegetables to the skillet; cook and stir until slightly tender, about three minutes. Stir flank steak in to the vegetable mixture; cook and stir before beef is cooked through, about five minutes.

Step three 3 Mix soy sauce, brown sugar, oyster sauce, and chile paste together in a little bowl; pour over the spaghetti. Dump spaghetti and sauce mixture in to the wok with the vegetables and steak; cook and stir before spaghetti is hot, 2-3 3 minutes.

09. Beef Lo Mein Recipe

Ingredients

1 (8-ounce) package spaghetti
1 teaspoon dark sesame oil
1 tablespoon peanut oil
4 cloves garlic, minced
1 tablespoon minced fresh ginger root
4 cups mixed vegetables
1 pound flank steak, thinly sliced
3 tablespoons reduced-sodium soy sauce
2 tablespoons brown sugar
1 tablespoon oyster sauces
1 tablespoon asian chile paste with garlic

Directions

Step 1 1 Bring a big pot of lightly salted water to a boil. Cook spaghetti in the boiling water until cooked through but firm to the bite, about 12 minutes; drain and transfer to a big bowl. Drizzle sesame oil over the spaghetti; toss to coat. Place a plate atop the bowl to keep carefully the noodles warm.

Step two 2 Heat peanut oil in a wok or large skillet over medium-high heat. Cook and stir garlic and ginger in hot oil until fragrant, about 30 seconds. Add mixed vegetables to the skillet; cook and stir until slightly tender, about three minutes. Stir flank steak in to the vegetable mixture; cook and stir before beef is cooked through, about five minutes.

Step three 3 Mix soy sauce, brown sugar, oyster sauce, and chile paste together in a little bowl; pour over the spaghetti. Dump spaghetti and sauce mixture in to the wok with the vegetables and steak; cook and stir before spaghetti is hot, 2-3 3 minutes.

10. Beef mince chow mein

Ingredients

600 g lan beef mince
1 1/5 medium brown onions, finely chopped
1 tablespoon curry powder, mild variety
1 1/5 large carrot(s), grated
450 g cabbage, savoy, raw, (1/4 small) white, finely shredded
2 2/5 individual celery, finely chopped
48 g rice, white, dry, (2tbs) long grain variety
96 g powdered chicken noodle soup, (2x40g pkts), reduced-salt variety
2 tablespoons soy sauce
180 g green beans, frozen, sliced
1 1/5 x 3 second spray(s) oils spray

Directions

Lightly spray a big saucepan with oil and heat over high temperature. Add mince and onion. Cook, splitting up any lumps, for 6-8 minutes or until mince has browned

Add curry powder and cook, stirring, for 1 minute or until fragrant. Add carrot, cabbage, celery, rice, soup mix, soy sauce and 2 cups (500ml) water and bring to the boil. Reduce heat and simmer, covered, for 20 minutes or until water has absorbed and rice is tender. Add beans going back 2 minutes of cooking. Serve.

SERVING SUGGESTION: steamed Asian greens, such as for example baby bok choy or choy sum. TIP: You may use lean chicken mince rather than beef.

11. Beef Stir-Fry Recipe

Ingredients

2 tablespoons vegetable oil
1 pound beef sirloin, cut into 2-inch strips
1 1/2 cups fresh broccoli florets
1 red bell pepper, cut into matchsticks
2 medium (blank)s carrots, thinly sliced
1 green onion, chopped
1 teaspoon minced garlic
2 tablespoons soy sauce
2 tablespoons sesame seeds, toasted

Directions

Step 1 Heat vegetable oil in a large wok or skillet over medium-high heat; cook and stir beef until browned, 3 to 4 minutes. Move beef to the side of the wok and add broccoli, bell pepper, carrots, green onion, and garlic to the center of the wok. Cook and stir vegetables for 2 minutes.

Step 2 Stir beef into vegetables and season with soy sauce and sesame seeds. Continue to cook and stir until vegetables are tender, about 2 more minutes.

12. Beef with Vegetables

Ingredients

8 ounces beef filet, cut into 1/2 inch strips
2 tablespoons vegetable oil
1 onion, chopped
1 clove garlic, minced
1 teaspoon chopped fresh ginger root
1 green bell pepper, chopped
1 carrot, chopped
1 (10.5 ounce) can beef broth
1 tablespoon cornstarch
1 teaspoon white sugar
1 tablespoon soy sauce
1 tablespoon oyster sauces
salt and pepper to taste

Directions

Step 1 1 In a big skillet over medium high temperature, saute the beef slices in the oil for five minutes, or until well browned. Add the onion, garlic and ginger and saute for 5 more minutes. Then add the green bell pepper, carrot and beef broth. Reduce heat to low and let simmer.

Step two 2 Meanwhile, in another normal size bowl, combine the corn flour, sugar, soy sauce and oyster sauce, if desired. Stir thoroughly, forming a smooth paste. Slowly add this to the simmering beef and vegetables, stirring well, and let simmer to desired thickness. Season with salt and pepper to taste.

13. Beef with Vegetables Recipe

Ingredients

8 ounces beef filet, cut into 1/2 inch strips
2 tablespoons vegetable oil
1 onion, chopped
1 clove garlic, minced
1 teaspoon chopped fresh ginger root
1 green bell pepper, chopped
1 carrot, chopped
1 (10.5 ounce) can beef broth
1 tablespoon cornstarch
1 teaspoon white sugar
1 tablespoon soy sauce
1 tablespoon oyster sauces
salt and pepper to taste

Directions

Step one 1 1 In a big skillet over medium temperature, saute the beef slices in the oil for 5 minutes, or until well browned. Add the onion, garlic and ginger and saute for 5 more minutes. Then add the green bell pepper, carrot and beef broth. Reduce heat to low and let simmer.

Second step 2 Meanwhile, in another normal size bowl, combine the corn flour, sugar, soy sauce and oyster sauce, if desired. Stir thoroughly, forming a smooth paste. Slowly add this to the simmering beef and vegetables, stirring well, and let simmer to desired thickness. Season with salt and pepper to taste.

14. Beefy Chinese Dumplings

Ingredients

1 3/4 pounds ground beef
2 1/3 cups shredded chinese cabbage
1 1/5 carrots, shredded
1 1/5 onions, minced
1 1/5 eggs
1 3/16 teaspoons sugar
1 3/16 teaspoons salt
1 tablespoon soy sauce
1 tablespoon vegetable oil
1 1/5 (14-ounce) packages wonton wrappers

Directions

Step 1 1 In a big bowl, mix together beef, cabbage, carrot, and onion. Stir in the egg, sugar, salt, soy sauce, and vegetable oil.

Step 2 2 Place a big teaspoonful of filling in the guts of a dumpling skin. Moisten the edges of a wonton with a few drops of water. Then fold the dumpling in two, and pinch the edges together to seal. Create a ripple pattern along the pinched edge by pinching and gently pushing together small segments of it. Repeat with remaining dumplings.

Step three 3 Boil the dumplings in water until they float to the most notable, about 5 minutes.

15. Bitter Melon and Black Bean Sauce Beef

Ingredients

1 ice cubes
1 bitter melon, seeded and sliced
2 teaspoons soy sauces, divided
2 teaspoons cornstarch, divided
1/4 teaspoon baking soda
6 ounces beef, sliced
1 tablespoon oils
1 teaspoon oils
1/2 onion, sliced
2 cloves garlic
1 tablespoon chopped fresh ginger
1 tablespoon black bean sauces
1 tablespoon oyster sauces
1 pinch white sugar, or to taste
3/4 cup water
1 teaspoon water
1 pinch salt to taste

Directions

Step one 1 Fill a bowl with ice; add enough salted water to create an ice bath. Bring a big pot of lightly salted water to a boil. Cook the bitter melon in the boiling water until tender yet firm, about 2 minutes; strain the melon. Place the melon in to the ice bath; allow to sit until bitterness is extracted, about one hour. Drain melon.

Step two 2 Whisk 1 teaspoon soy sauce, 1 teaspoon cornstarch, and baking soda together in a bowl. Add beef and toss to evenly coat. Marinate in the refrigerator for one hour.

Step three 3 Heat wok, or a big skillet, on high until smoking. Add 1 tablespoon oil. Lay beef evenly over the bottom of the wok; cook until browned, about 2 minutes per side. Remove beef. Pour in 1 teaspoon of oil; allow to heat. Add onion, garlic, and ginger; cook and stir until fragrant, about 30 seconds. Stir in bitter melon; cook until combined, about 1 minute.

Step 4 Stir black bean sauce into melon mixture. Stir in remaining soy sauce, oyster sauce, and sugar. Pour in 3/4 cup water; cover and let simmer until flavors combine, 2-3 three minutes. Uncover and mix in remaining cornstarch and 1 teaspoon water and stir until thickened.

16. Black Pepper Beef and Cabbage Stir Fry

Ingredients

2 tablespoons vegetable oil
4 cloves garlic, chopped
1/2 pound ground beef
1/2 small head cabbage, shredded
1 red bell pepper, cut into strips
2 tablespoons soy sauce
1 teaspoon cornstarch
1/2 cup cold water
1 teaspoon ground black pepper, or to taste
1 pinch salt, to taste

Directions

The first step 1 Heat a wok or large skillet over medium-high heat, and add oil. Saute garlic for about 5 seconds, then add ground beef. Stir-fry until beef is evenly brown, 5 to 7 minutes; drain body fat.

Second step 2 Stir in cabbage and pepper, and cook until vegetables are tender and beef is fully cooked. Stir in soy sauce. Mix together cornstarch and water, and stir in. Season with pepper; add salt to taste. Cook, stirring, until sauce has thickened.

17. Chicken and Chinese Vegetable Stir-Fry

Ingredients

14 ounces skinless, boneless chicken breasts meat - cut into bite-size pieces
1/2 cup oyster sauces
2 tablespoons soy sauce
3 tablespoons vegetable oil
2 cloves garlic, minced
1 large onion, chopped
1/2 cup water
1 teaspoon ground black pepper
1 teaspoon white sugar
1 (8-ounce) can sliced water chestnuts, drained
1 cup snow peas
1 small head broccoli, cut into florets
3 tablespoons cornstarch
1/4 cup water

Directions

Step one 1 Combine the chicken, oyster sauce, and soy sauce in a mixing bowl before chicken is evenly coated with the sauce; reserve.

Step two 2 Heat the vegetable oil in a wok or large skillet over high temperature. Stir in the garlic and onion; cook and stir before onion is limp, about 1 minute. Add the chicken and marinade. Cook and stir before chicken has browned and is no more pink, about 10 minutes.

Step three 3 Pour in 1/2 cup of water; season with pepper and sugar. Add the water chestnuts, snow peas, and broccoli. Cover; boil before vegetables are simply tender, about five minutes. Dissolve the cornstarch in 1/4 cup of water. Stir in to the boiling mixture; cook until thick no longer cloudy.

18. Chicken Broccoli Ca - Unieng's Style

Ingredients

12 ounces boneless, skinless chicken breasts halves, cut into bite-sized pieces
1 tablespoon oyster sauces
2 tablespoons dark soy sauce
3 tablespoons vegetable oil
2 cloves garlic, chopped
1 large onion, cut into rings
1/2 cup water
1 teaspoon ground black pepper
1 teaspoon white sugar
1/2 medium head bok choy, chopped
1 small head broccoli, chopped
1 tablespoon cornstarch, mixed with equal parts water

Directions

In a big bowl, combine chicken, oyster sauce and soy sauce. Reserve for 15 minutes.

Heat oil in a wok or large heavy skillet over medium heat. Saute garlic and onion until soft and translucent. Increase heat to high. Add chicken and marinade, then stir-fry until light golden brown, about ten minutes. Stir in water, pepper and sugar. Add bok choy and broccoli, and cook stirring until soft, about ten minutes. Pour in the cornstarch mixture, and cook until sauce is thickened, about five minutes.

19. Chinese Barbeque Pork (Char Siu)

Ingredients

2/3 cup soy sauce
1/2 cup honey
1/2 cup chinese rice wine (or sake or dry sherry)
1/3 cup hoisin sauce
1/3 cup ketchup
1/3 cup brown sugar
4 cloves garlic, crushed
1 teaspoon chinese five-spice powder
1/2 teaspoon freshly ground black pepper
1/4 teaspoon cayenne pepper
1/8 teaspoon pink curing salt (optional)
1 (3 pound) boneless pork butt (shoulder)
1 teaspoon red food coloring, or as desired (optional)
1 teaspoon kosher salt, or to taste

Directions

Place soy sauce, honey, rice wine, hoisin sauce, ketchup, brown sugar, garlic, five-spice powder, black pepper, cayenne pepper, and curing salt in a saucepan. Bring to a boil on high temperature; reduce heat to medium-high. Cook for 1 minute. Remove from heat. Cool to room temperature.

Cut pork roast in two lengthwise. Cut each half again lengthwise forming 4 long, thick bits of pork.

Transfer cooled sauce to a big mixing bowl. Stir in red food coloring. Place pork sections into sauce and coat each piece. Cover with plastic wrap and refrigerate 4 to 12 hours.

Preheat grill for medium heat, 275 to 300 degrees F (135 to 150 degrees C) and lightly oil the grate. Line a baking sheet with parchment paper.

Remove parts of pork from marinade and let excess drip off. Put on prepared baking sheet. Sprinkle with kosher salt to taste.

Transfer pork sections to grate over indirect heat on prepared grill. Cover and cook about 45 minutes. Brush with marinade; turn. Continue cooking until an instant-read thermometer inserted in to the center reads 185 and 190 degrees F, about one hour and 15 minutes more. Usually do not use any longer marinade on cooked meat until once you boil it.

Place leftover marinade in saucepan; bring to a boil; let simmer 1 minutes. Remove from heat. You can now utilize it to brush over the cooked pork.

20. Chinese Beef and Broccoli Recip

Ingredients

1 pound flank steak (sliced thin crosswise)
1 1/2 pounds broccoli (cut into florets (discard stems or save for another use))
1 tablespoon vegetable oil
1 2-inch piece of fresh ginger, minced
3 cloves garlic (minced)
2 tablespoons cornstarch
1 tablespoon soy sauce
2 teaspoons rice vinegar
1/2 teaspoon sesame oil
8 tablespoons water
2 tablespoons soy sauce
2 tablespoons oyster sauces
2 teaspoons cornstarch
1 teaspoon dark brown sugar
1/2 teaspoon sesame oil

Directions

In a little bowl, whisk together each of the marinade Ingredients. Pour it right into a gallon-size resealable plastic bag, add the beef, seal the bag and transform it so that all the bits of the beef are coated in the marinade. Allow to rest at room temperature for a quarter-hour.

Meanwhile, place 1 inch of water in a big sauté pan and bring to a boil over high temperature. Add the broccoli, cover and steam for three minutes. Drain the broccoli and reserve.

Wipe the pan dry and stick it over medium-high heat. Once hot, add the vegetable oil and quickly swirl it to coat the pan. Add the beef in as a good layer as possible, taking care never to overlap the pieces an excessive amount of. Cook before edges are browning, 30 seconds to at least one 1 minute, then flip over. Add the garlic and ginger and commence to toss the beef mixture in a "stir-fry" fashion until no pink remains.

Take away the beef from the pan with a slotted spoon and place in a bowl. Whisk together the sauce Ingredients and enhance the pan, whisking and stirring before sauce has thickened, about one to two 2 minutes. Decrease the heat to low, add back the beef and broccoli to the pan and stir to coat it with the sauce. Serve immediately over white rice.

21. Chinese Beef With Broccoli

Ingredients

2 tablespoons cornstarch
4 tablespoons soy sauce
2 teaspoons sugar
5 tablespoons peanut oil
1 pound flank steak, thinly sliced against the grain
1 tablespoon oyster sauces
1 1/4 cups low-sodium chicken broth
4 thin slices peeled ginger
1 head broccoli, cut into florets
1 large onion, halved and sliced 1/2 inch thick
3 plum tomatoes, quartered lengthwise
2 cloves garlic, minced
cooked white rice, for serving (optional)

Directions

Whisk 1 tablespoon cornstarch, 3 tablespoons soy sauce, 1 teaspoon sugar and 1 tablespoon peanut oil in a big bowl. Add the steak and toss to coat; refrigerate until prepared to cook.

Whisk the rest of the 1 tablespoon each cornstarch and soy sauce, the oyster sauce and chicken broth in a little bowl; set aside.

Heat 1 tablespoon peanut oil in a big skillet over high temperature. Add the ginger, broccoli and the rest of the 1 teaspoon sugar and stir-fry three to four 4 minutes; transfer to a plate. Heat 1 more tablespoon peanut oil in the skillet, add the onion and stir-fry 2-3 three minutes. Add the tomatoes and cook, turning gently, 2 minutes. Transfer the onion and tomatoes to the plate with the broccoli.

Decrease the heat to medium high; add the rest of the 2 tablespoons peanut oil to the skillet. Add the garlic and steak and stir-fry 1 minute. Whisk the sauce mixture, then enhance the skillet and simmer 1 minute. Return the vegetables to the skillet; cook before meat is cooked through, three to four 4 minutes. Serve with rice, if desired.

22. Chinese Chicken Fried Rice

Ingredients

1/2 tablespoon sesame oil
1 onion
1 1/2 pounds cooked, cubed chicken meat
2 tablespoons soy sauce
2 large carrots, diced
2 stalks celery, chopped
1 large red bell pepper, diced
3/4 cup fresh pea pods, halved
1/2 large green bell pepper, diced
6 cups cooked white rice
2 large eggs eggs
1/3 cup soy sauce

Directions

Step one 1 Heat oil in a big skillet over medium heat. Add onion and saute until soft, then add chicken and 2 tablespoons soy sauce and stir-fry for 5 to 6 minutes.

Step two 2 Stir in carrots, celery, red bell pepper, pea pods and green bell pepper and stir-fry another five minutes. Then add rice and stir thoroughly.

Step three 3 Finally, stir in scrambled eggs and 1/3 cup soy sauce, heat through and serve hot.

23. Chinese Ginger & Horseradish Beef

Ingredients

1 1/4 pounds beef sirloin (thinly sliced)
3 1/5 large scallions (1.5" slices)
2 3/8 teaspoons fresh ginger
1 tablespoon dijon mustard
2 3/8 teaspoons honey
3 tablespoons soy sauce
3 tablespoons water
3/16 teaspoon kosher salt
3/8 teaspoon ground black pepper
3 tablespoons canola oil

Directions

In a medium bowl, combine beef and scallions.

To a blender, add all remaining Ingredients, except oil. Blend until smooth.

Combine beef and marinade thoroughly. Let marinate in refrigerator for 4-6 hours.

To a big skillet over high temperature, add oil. When hot, add marinated beef. Stir fry for 5-7 minutes or until beef is cooked through. You will have a whole lot of moisture released from the meat. Cook until liquid is nearly fully cooked out.

24. Chinese Noodle Chicken Recipe

Ingredients

4 breast half, bone and skin removed (blank)s skinless, boneless chicken breasts
1 tablespoon vegetable oil
1/2 cup sliced onions
2 cups broccoli florets
2 medium (blank)s carrots, julienned
2 cups snow peas
4 cups dry chinese noodles
1/4 cup teriyaki sauce

Directions

Step 1 1 In a big skillet brown chicken in oil, stirring constantly until juices run clear.

Step two 2 Add the onion, broccoli, carrots and peas. Cover skillet and steam for 2 minutes.

Step three 3 Add the Chinese noodles and teriyaki sauce. Stir noodles into chicken/vegetable mixture, making sure they are coated with sauce. When the noodles wilt, serve.

25. Chinese Pepper Steak Recipe

Ingredients

1 3/4 pounds beef top sirloin steak
7 tablespoons soy sauce
3 1/2 tablespoons white sugar
3 1/2 tablespoons cornstarch
7/8 teaspoon ground ginger
5 tablespoons vegetable oil, divided
1 3/4 red onions, cut into 1-inch squares
1 3/4 green bell pepper, cut into 1-inch squares
3 1/2 tomatoes tomatoes, cut into wedges

Directions

Step 1 1 Cut the steak into 1/2-inch thick slices over the grain.

Step two 2 Whisk together soy sauce, sugar, cornstarch, and ginger in a bowl before sugar has dissolved and the mixture is smooth. Place the steak slices in to the marinade, and stir until well-coated.

Step three 3 Heat 1 tablespoon of vegetable oil in a wok or large skillet over medium-high heat, and place 1/3 of the steak strips in to the hot oil. Cook and stir before beef is well-browned, about three minutes, and take away the beef from the wok to a bowl. Repeat twice more, with the rest of the beef, and set the cooked beef aside.

Step 4 4 Return all of the cooked beef to the hot wok, and stir in the onion. Toss the beef and onion together before onion begins to soften, about 2 minutes, then stir in the green pepper. Cook and stir the mixture before pepper has turned bright green and began to become tender, about 2 minutes, then add the tomatoes, stir everything together, and serve.

26. Chinese Pork Tenderloin

Ingredients

2 (1 1/2 pound) pork tenderloins, trimmed
2 tablespoons light soy sauce
2 tablespoons hoisin sauce
1 tablespoon sherry
1 tablespoon black bean sauces
1 1/2 teaspoons minced fresh ginger root
1 1/2 teaspoons packed brown sugar
1 clove garlic
1/2 teaspoon sesame oil
1 pinch chinese five-spice powder

Directions

Place tenderloins in a shallow glass dish. In a little bowl, whisk together soy sauce, hoisin sauce, sherry, black bean sauce, ginger, sugar, garlic, sesame oil, and five-spice powder. Pour marinade over pork, and turn to coat. Cover, and refrigerate for at least 2 hours or up to a day.

Preheat oven to 375 degrees F (190 degrees C). Remove tenderloins from refrigerator as the oven preheats.

Bake pork in preheated oven for 30 to 35 minutes, or even to desired doneness. Let are a symbol of 10 minutes, and slice diagonally into thin slices.

27. Chinese Roast Pork

Ingredients

4 pounds bone-in pork roast
3/4 cup soy sauce
1/2 cup dry sherry
1/3 cup honey
2 cloves garlic, minced
1/2 teaspoon ground ginger
1 tablespoon cornstarch
1 tablespoon water

Directions

Step one 1 To Marinate: Pierce meaty sides of meat with fork; place roast in a big plastic bag. In a medium bowl combine the soy sauce, sherry, honey, garlic and ginger. Mix well and pour mixture into bag with pork. Press air out from the bag and tie securely. Refrigerate at least 8 hours or overnight, turning bag over occasionally.

Step two 2 Preheat oven to 325 degrees F (165 degrees C).

Step three 3 Remove roast and marinade from refrigerator. Reserving marinade, remove roast and place in a 9x13 inch baking dish. Roast in the preheated oven for one hour. Brush with reserved marinade; cover loosely with foil and roast for yet another 1 1/2 hours (or before internal temperature has already reached 145 degrees F (63 degrees C), brushing many times with marinade.

Step 4 Remove roast from oven and let stand quarter-hour. Combine pan drippings with remaining marinade. In a little bowl combine cornstarch with cool water, mix together and add mixture to marinade. Boil marinade mixture for 4 to five minutes, or until mixture thickens. Serve with roast.

28. Chinese Spareribs Recipe

Ingredients

6 tablespoons hoisin sauce
2 tablespoons ketchup
2 tablespoons honey
2 tablespoons soy sauce
2 tablespoons sake
2 teaspoons rice vinegar
2 teaspoons lemon juice
2 teaspoons grated fresh ginger
1 teaspoon grated fresh garlic
1/2 teaspoon chinese five-spice powder
2 pounds pork spareribs

Directions

Step one 1 In a shallow glass dish, mix together the hoisin sauce, ketchup, honey, soy sauce, sake, rice vinegar, lemon juice, ginger, garlic and five-spice powder. Place the ribs in the dish, and turn to coat. Cover and marinate in the refrigerator for 2 hours, or given that overnight.

Step two 2 Preheat the oven to 325 degrees F (165 degrees C). Fill a broiler tray with enough water to cover underneath. Place the grate or rack over the tray. Arrange the ribs on the grate.

Step three 3 Place the broiler rack in the heart of the oven. Cook for 40 minutes, turning and brushing with the marinade every ten minutes. Allow marinade cook on for the ultimate 10 minutes to generate a glaze. Finish beneath the broiler if desired. Discard any remaining marinade.

29. Crispy Ginger Beef

Ingredients

1 cup cornstarch
2/3 cup water
2 4/5 large eggs eggs
1 1/3 pounds flank steak, cut into thin strips
2/3 cup canola oils, or as needed
1 2/5 large carrots, cut into matchstick-size pieces
1 2/5 green bell pepper, cut into matchstick-size pieces
1 2/5 red bell pepper, cut into matchstick-size pieces
4 1/5 eaches green onions, chopped
5 1/2 tablespoons minced fresh ginger root
7 eaches garlic cloves, minced
2/3 cup white sugar
5 1/2 tablespoons rice vinegar
1/4 cup soy sauce
1 1/2 tablespoons sesame oil
1 1/2 tablespoons red pepper flakes, or to taste

Directions

Step one 1 Place cornstarch in a big bowl; gradually whisk in water until smooth. Whisk eggs into cornstarch mixture; toss steak strips in mixture to coat.

Step two 2 Pour canola oil into wok 1-inch deep; heat oil over high temperature until hot however, not smoking. Place 1/4 of the beef strips into hot oil; separate strips with a fork. Cook, stirring frequently, until coating is crisp and golden, about three minutes. Remove beef to drain in writing towels; repeat with remaining beef.

Step three 3 Drain off all but 1 tablespoon oil; cook and stir carrot, green bell pepper, red bell pepper, green onions, ginger, and garlic over high temperature until lightly browned but nonetheless crisp, about 3 minutes.

Step 4 Whisk sugar, rice vinegar, soy sauce, sesame oil, and red pepper together in a little bowl. Pour sauce mixture over vegetables in wok; bring mixture to a boil. Stir beef back to vegetable mixture; cook and stir just until heated through, about three minutes.

30. Crispy Orange Beef

Ingredients

1 1/2 pounds beef top sirloin, thinly sliced
1/3 cup white sugar
1/3 cup rice wine vinegar
2 tablespoons frozen orange juice concentrate
1 teaspoon salt
1 tablespoon soy sauce
1 cup long grain rice
2 cups water
1/4 cup cornstarch
2 teaspoons orange zest
3 tablespoons grated fresh ginger
1 1/2 tablespoons minced garlic
8 stalks (blank)s broccoli florets, lightly steamed or blanched
2 cups oils for frying

Directions

Step one 1 Lay beef strips out within a layer on a baking sheet lined with paper towels. Allow to dry in the refrigerator for thirty minutes. In a little bowl, mix together the sugar, rice vinegar, orange juice concentrate, salt and soy sauce. Reserve.

Step two 2 Meanwhile, combine rice and water in a medium saucepan. Bring to a boil, then reduce heat to medium-low and simmer for 20 minutes, or until rice is tender. Add more water towards the end if necessary.

Step three 3 Heat oil in a wok over medium-high heat. Toss dried beef in cornstarch to coat. Fry in the hot oil in small batches until crispy and golden brown; reserve. Drain each of the oil from the wok except about 1 tablespoon.

Step 4 Add orange zest, ginger and garlic to the rest of the oil, and cook briefly until fragrant. Add the soy sauce mixture to the wok, bring to a boil, and cook until thick and syrupy, about five minutes. Add beef, and heat through, stirring to coat. Serve immediately over steamed rice, and garnish with broccoli.

31. Crispy Orange Beef Recipes

Ingredients

1 1/2 pounds beef top sirloin, thinly sliced
1/3 cup white sugar
1/3 cup rice wine vinegar
2 tablespoons frozen orange juice concentrate
1 teaspoon salt
1 tablespoon soy sauce
1 cup long grain rice
2 cups water
1/4 cup cornstarch
2 teaspoons orange zest
3 tablespoons grated fresh ginger
1 1/2 tablespoons minced garlic
8 stalks (blank)s broccoli florets, lightly steamed or blanched
2 cups oils for frying

Directions

Step one 1 Lay beef strips out in one layer on a baking sheet lined with paper towels. Allow to dry in the refrigerator for thirty minutes. In a little bowl, mix together the sugar, rice vinegar, orange juice concentrate, salt and soy sauce. Reserve.

Step two 2 Meanwhile, combine rice and water in a medium saucepan. Bring to a boil, then reduce heat to medium-low and simmer for 20 minutes, or until rice is tender. Add more water by the end if necessary.

Step three 3 Heat oil in a wok over medium-high heat. Toss dried beef in cornstarch to coat. Fry in the hot oil in small batches until crispy and golden brown; reserve. Drain all the oil from the wok except about 1 tablespoon.

Step 4 Add orange zest, ginger and garlic to the rest of the oil, and cook briefly until fragrant. Add the soy sauce mixture to the wok, bring to a boil, and cook until thick and syrupy, about five minutes. Add beef, and heat through, stirring to coat. Serve immediately over steamed rice, and garnish with broccoli.

32. Eggplant with Garlic Sauce

Ingredients

1/4 cup canola oil
5 1/3 eggplant, unpeeled (approx 1.25 lbs)s chinese eggplants, halved lengthwise and cut into 1 inch half moons
1 1/3 cups water
1 1/2 tablespoons crushed red pepper flakes
1/4 cup garlic powder
2 tablespoons white sugar
1 1/3 teaspoons cornstarch
2 1/2 tablespoons light soy sauce
2 1/2 tablespoons oyster sauces

Directions

Step one 1 Heat the canola oil in a skillet over high temperature. Cook and stir the eggplant until soft, about 4 minutes. Stir in the water, red pepper flakes, and garlic powder. Cover and simmer until all of the water is absorbed. Meanwhile, mix sugar, cornstarch, soy sauce, and oyster sauce in a bowl until sugar and cornstarch have dissolved. Stir sauce in to the eggplant, making sure to evenly coat the eggplant. Cook before sauce has thickened.

33. Flavorful Beef Stir-Fry

Ingredients

2 cups brown rice brown rice
4 cups water water
2 tablespoons cornstarch cornstarch
2 teaspoons sugar white sugar
6 tablespoons soy sauce soy sauce
1/4 cup white wine white wine
1 tablespoon ginger minced fresh ginger
1 pound beef round steaks boneless beef round steak cut into thin strips
1 tablespoon vegetable oil vegetable oil
3 cups broccoli broccoli florets
2 carrots medium (blank)s carrots thinly sliced
1 package pea pods (6 ounce) frozen pea pods thawed
2 tablespoons onions chopped onion
1 can water chestnuts (8 ounce) sliced water chestnuts undrained
1 cup chinese cabbage Chinese cabbage
2 heads bok choy large bok choy

chopped
1 tablespoon vegetable oil vegetable oil

Directions

Step one 1 Bring brown rice and water to a boil in a saucepan over high temperature. Reduce heat to medium-low, cover, and simmer until rice is tender, and liquid has been absorbed, 45 to 50 minutes.

Step two 2 Combine cornstarch, sugar, soy sauce, and wine in a little bowl until smooth. Stir in ginger; toss beef in sauce to coat.

Step three 3 Heat 1 tablespoon oil in a big skillet over medium-high heat. Cook and stir broccoli, carrots, pea pods, and onion for 1 minute. Stir in water chestnuts, Chinese cabbage, and bok choy; cover and simmer until vegetables are tender, about 4 minutes. Remove from skillet and keep warm.

Step 4 In same skillet, heat 1 tablespoon oil over medium-high heat. Cook and stir beef until desired amount of doneness, about 2 minutes per side for medium. Return vegetables to skillet; cook and stir until heated through, about three minutes. Serve over rice.

34. General Tso's Chicken Recipe

Ingredients

5 1/3 cups vegetable oil for frying
4 large eggs eggs
2/3 cup cornstarch
1 1/3 pounds skinless, boneless chicken thighs, cut into bite-sized pieces
1 1/2 tablespoons vegetable oil
6 2/3 pepper s dried red pepper pods
2 tablespoons rice vinegar
2 1/2 tablespoons rice wine
1/4 cup white sugar
1/4 cup soy sauce
2 2/3 teaspoons cornstarch
4 eaches green onions, thinly sliced

Directions

The first step 1 Heat oil in a deep-fryer or large saucepan to 375 degrees F (190 degrees C).

Second step 2 Beat the eggs in a mixing bowl until smooth. Stir in 1/2 cup of cornstarch until no lumps remain, then mix in the chicken until evenly coated in batter.

Third step 3 In batches, carefully drop the chicken cubes into the hot oil individually, cooking before chicken turns golden brown and begins to float, around three minutes. Drain on a paper towel-lined plate.

Step 4 Heat the vegetable oil in a wok or large skillet over temperature. Stir in the dried peppers, and cook for about 30 seconds before color brightens. Add the chicken, and cook for a couple minutes before chicken turns a deep, golden brown. Stir the vinegar, rice wine, sugar, soy sauce, and 2 teaspoons of cornstarch together in just a little bowl. Pour into the wok, and boil before sauce thickens and is forget about cloudy, about 2 minutes. Garnish with green onions to serve.

35. Grilled Asian Chicken Recipe

Ingredients

1/4 cup soy sauce
4 teaspoons sesame oil
2 tablespoons honey
3 slices fresh ginger root
2 cloves garlic, crushed
4 breast half, bone and skin removed (blank)s skinless, boneless chicken breasts halves

Directions

Step 1 1 In a little microwave-safe bowl, combine the soy sauce, oil, honey, ginger root, and garlic. Heat in microwave on medium for 1 minute, then stir. Heat again for 30 seconds, watching closely to avoid boiling.

Step two 2 Place chicken breasts in a shallow dish. Pour soy sauce mixture over, and reserve to marinate for quarter-hour.

Step three 3 Preheat a grill for medium-high heat. Drain marinade from chicken right into a small saucepan. Bring to a boil, and simmer over medium heat for five minutes. Set aside for basting.

Step 4 Lightly oil the grill grate. Cook chicken on the prepared grill six to eight 8 minutes per side, or until juices run clear. Baste frequently with remaining marinade. Chicken will turn a lovely golden brown.

36. Grilled Hoisin Beef Recipe

Ingredients

1 (1 pound) beef skirt steak
1/3 cup hoisin sauce
3 tablespoons chinese vinegar (or sherry vinegar)
1 tablespoon soy sauce
2 teaspoons hot sauce
2 teaspoons sesame oil
1 tablespoon grated fresh ginger root
4 cloves garlic, finely minced
1 tablespoon packed brown sugar
1 teaspoon salt
1/2 teaspoon freshly ground black pepper
1 green onion, light parts only, minced
1 teaspoon toasted sesame seeds

Directions

Step one 1 Whisk hoisin sauce, vinegar, soy sauce, hot sauce, sesame oil, grated ginger, garlic, brown sugar, salt, and pepper together in a big mixing bowl.

Step two 2 Cut skirt steak crosswise into about four or five 5 smaller pieces. Transfer steak into marinade and toss until all pieces are evenly coated. Cover with plastic wrap. Refrigerate; marinate at least 2 hours or more to 12 hours.

Step three 3 Line a baking pan with paper towels. Transfer bits of steak to the paper towels and mop off a number of the marinade.

Step 4 4 Preheat a patio grill for high temperature and lightly oil the grate.

Step 5 Transfer steak pieces to grill. Cook to medium rare or medium, 4 to five minutes per side. An instant-read thermometer inserted in to the center should read between 130 and 135 degrees F (about 54 degrees C). Thinner pieces might finish earlier. Transfer steak to a warm plate. Let rest for a couple minutes.

Step 6 Transfer steak to a warm serving platter and pour any accumulated juices over skirt steak. Sprinkle with sesame seeds and sliced green onions.

37. Honey Walnut Shrimp Recipe

Ingredients

1 cup water
2/3 cup white sugar
1/2 cup walnuts
4 large eggs whites egg whites
2/3 cup mochiko (glutinous rice flour)
1/4 cup mayonnaise
1 pound large shrimp, peeled and deveined
2 tablespoons honey
1 tablespoon canned sweetened condensed milk
1 cup vegetable oil for frying

Directions

Step one 1 Stir together the water and sugar in a little saucepan. Bring to a boil and add the walnuts. Boil for 2 minutes, then drain and place wa°Step one 1 Stir together the water and sugar in a little saucepan. Bring to a boil and add the walnuts. Boil for 2 minutes, then drain and place walnuts on a cookie sheet to dry.

Step two 2 Whip egg whites in a medium bowl until foamy. Stir in the mochiko until it includes a pasty consistency. Heat the oil in much deep skillet over medium-high heat. Dip shrimp in to the mochiko batter, and fry in the hot oil until golden brown, about five minutes. Remove with a slotted spoon and drain in writing towels.

Step three 3 In a medium serving bowl, stir together the mayonnaise, honey and sweetened condensed milk. Add shrimp and toss to coat with the sauce. Sprinkle the candied walnuts at the top and serve.

lnuts on a cookie sheet to dry.

Step two 2 Whip egg whites in a medium bowl until foamy. Stir in the mochiko until it includes a pasty consistency. Heat the oil in much deep skillet over medium-high heat. Dip shrimp in to the mochiko batter, and fry in the hot oil until golden brown, about five minutes. Remove with a slotted spoon and drain in writing towels.

Step three 3 In a medium serving bowl, stir together the mayonnaise, honey and sweetened condensed milk. Add shrimp and toss to coat with the sauce. Sprinkle the candied walnuts at the top and serve.

38. Hot and Tangy Broccoli Beef

Ingredients

3/4 pound boneless tender beef steak, rib eye, sirloin or flank
1 tablespoon cornstarch
3 tablespoons kikkoman soy sauces, divided
1 large clove garlic, minced
1/2 teaspoon sugar
1 pound fresh broccoli, trimmed
4 teaspoons cornstarch
1/2 teaspoon crushed red pepper
3 tablespoons vegetable oil, divided
1 medium onion, thinly sliced
2 teaspoons kikkoman seasoned rice vinegar

Directions

Cut beef across grain into thin slices. Combine 1 Tbsp. each cornstarch and soy sauce with garlic and sugar in medium bowl; stir in beef. Let stand ten minutes.

Meanwhile, remove flowerets from broccoli; cut into bite-size pieces. Peel stalks; cut diagonally into thin slices.

Combine 1 cup water, remaining 2 Tbsp. soy sauce, 4 teaspoons cornstarch and crushed red pepper in normal size bowl. Set aside.

Heat 1 Tbsp. oil in hot wok or large skillet over high temperature. Add beef and stir-fry 1 minute; remove.

Heat remaining 2 Tbsp. oil in same pan. Add broccoli and onion; stir-fry 2 minutes. Sprinkle 1 Tbsp. water over vegetables; cover and cook 2 minutes, stirring occasionally.

Add beef and soy sauce mixture; cook and stir until sauce boils and thickens. Remove from heat; stir in vinegar.

39. Kikkoman Chinese Pepper Steak

Ingredients

1 pound boneless beef sirloin or round steak
1 tablespoon kikkoman hoisin sauce
2 tablespoons vegetable oil, divided
2 medium bell peppers, cut into 1-inch squares
2 medium onions, cut into 1-inch squares
1/4 cup kikkoman hoisin sauce

Directions

Cut steak across grain into thin strips, then into 1-inch squares; coat with 1 Tbsp. hoisin sauce.

Heat 1 Tbsp. oil in hot wok or large skillet over high temperature. Add beef and stir-fry about 1 minute; remove.

Heat remaining 1 Tbsp. oil in same pan. Add peppers and onions; stir-fry five minutes. Stir in beef and remaining 1/4 cup hoisin sauce; cook and stir just until beef and vegetables are coated with sauce. Serve immediately.

40. Kung Pao Chicken Recipe

Ingredients

1 1/2 pounds skinless, boneless chicken breasts halves - cut into chunks
3 tablespoons white wine
3 tablespoons soy sauce
3 tablespoons sesame oils, divided
3 tablespoons cornstarch, dissolved in 2 tablespoons water
1 1/2 ounces hot chile paste
1 1/2 teaspoons distilled white vinegar
1 tablespoon brown sugar
6 green onions, chopped
1 1/2 tablespoons chopped garlic
1 1/2 (8-ounce) cans water chestnuts
6 ounces chopped peanuts

Directions

TO CREATE Marinade: Combine 1 tablespoon wine, 1 tablespoon soy sauce, 1 tablespoon oil and 1 tablespoon cornstarch/water mixture and mix together. Place chicken pieces in a glass dish or bowl and add marinade. Toss to coat. Cover dish and place in refrigerator for approximately 30 minutes.

To Make Sauce: In a little bowl combine 1 tablespoon wine, 1 tablespoon soy sauce, 1 tablespoon oil, 1 tablespoon cornstarch/water mixture, chili paste, vinegar and sugar. Mix together and add green onion, garlic, water chestnuts and peanuts. In a medium skillet, heat sauce slowly until aromatic.

Meanwhile, remove chicken from marinade and saute in a big skillet until meat is white and juices run clear. When sauce is aromatic, add sauteed chicken to it and let simmer together until sauce thickens.

41. Ma Po Tofu Recipe

Ingredients

2 ounces ground pork
1 tablespoon dry sherry
1/2 teaspoon cornstarch
3/4 teaspoon fermented black beans, rinsed and mashed
3/4 teaspoon chili paste with garlic
1/2 teaspoon cayenne pepper
1 tablespoon soy sauce
1 1/2 tablespoons garlic, crushed
1/4 teaspoon minced fresh ginger
1/2 (14-ounce) package tofu, drained and cut into cubes
1/2 cup frozen green peas
1/4 cup chicken broth
1 1/2 teaspoons cornstarch, mixed with equal parts water

Directions

Step 1 1 In a little bowl, combine ground pork, sherry and 1 teaspoon cornstarch; reserve.

Step 2 2 In another normal size bowl, combine black beans, chile paste, cayenne pepper, soy sauce, garlic, and ginger; reserve.

Step 3 3 Heat a big skillet over medium heat. If pork is lean, add 1 tablespoon oil. Cook pork until evenly browned. Stir in black bean mixture, tofu, and peas. Pour in chicken broth, and bring to a boil. Stir in dissolved cornstarch, and cook until thickened.

42. Minchee (Chinese Beef & Potato Hash)

Ingredients

1 pound 80/20 ground beef
1 1/5 russet potatoes
3/10 white onion
1 1/5 bay leaves
1 1/4 teaspoons canola oil
1 1/4 teaspoons grated ginger
4 1/2 tablespoons grated garlic
3 1/2 tablespoons low sodium Worcestershire sauce
3 1/2 tablespoons soy sauce
1 1/2 dashes salt
4 4/5 green onions

Directions

Dice potato and white onion into 1/4-inch cubes.

Heat canola oil in a big saucepan over medium heat. Add white onion, bay leaf, and salt; cook 3-4 minutes. Add grated garlic and ginger; stir and cook yet another 1 minute.

Add beef to the saucepan and split up into small pieces. Cook about 2 minutes until broken and just starting to brown.

Add diced potato, Worcestershire sauce, and soy sauce and mix with beef/onions. Cover and cook over medium heat for 20 minutes.

Serve over rice and top with diced green onions.

43. Mongolian Beef

Ingredients

1 teaspoon sesame seeds
1 tablespoon soy sauce
1 tablespoon cornstarch
2 cloves garlic, minced
1 pound beef round steak, cut into thin strips
3/4 cup water
2 tablespoons soy sauce
2 1/2 teaspoons cornstarch
1/2 teaspoon white sugar
1 teaspoon red pepper flakes
2 tablespoons vegetable oil, divided
2 medium (blank)s carrots, thinly sliced
1 bunch green onions, cut into 2 inch pieces

Directions

Step one 1 In a dry skillet over medium heat, toast sesame seeds for 1 to2 minutes, or before seeds begin to carefully turn golden brown; set aside.

Step two 2 In a medium bowl, mix together 1 tablespoon soy sauce, 1 tablespoon cornstarch, and minced garlic. Stir in beef strips. Let are a symbol of at least 10 minutes.

Step 3 3 In another normal size bowl, mix together water, 2 tablespoons soy sauce, 2 1/2 teaspoons cornstarch, sugar, sesame seeds, and red pepper flakes; reserve.

Step 4 Heat 1 tablespoon of oil in a wok or skillet over high temperature. Cook and stir beef in hot oil for 1 minute; remove, and reserve. Heat remaining tablespoon of oil in the same pan. Saute carrots and white part of green onions for 2 minutes. Stir in green elements of the green onion, and saute for 1 minute. Stir in sesame seed mixture and beef. Cook and stir until sauce boils and thickens.

44. Mongolian Beef and Spring Onions

Ingredients

2 teaspoons vegetable oil
1 tablespoon finely chopped garlic
1/2 teaspoon grated fresh ginger root
1/2 cup soy sauce
1/2 cup water
2/3 cup dark brown sugar
1 pound beef flank steak, sliced 1/4 inch thick on the diagonal
1/4 cup cornstarch
1 cup vegetable oil for frying
2 bunches green onions, cut in 2-inch lengths

Directions

Step one 1 Heat 2 teaspoons of vegetable oil in a saucepan over medium heat, and cook and stir the garlic and ginger until they release their fragrance, about 30 seconds. Pour in the soy sauce, water, and brown sugar. Improve the heat to medium-high, and stir 4 minutes, before sugar has dissolved and the sauce boils and slightly thickens. Remove sauce from heat, and set aside.

Step two 2 Place the sliced beef right into a bowl, and stir the cornstarch in to the beef, coating it thoroughly. Permit the beef and cornstarch to sit until a lot of the juices from the meat have already been absorbed by the cornstarch, about ten minutes.

Step three 3 Heat the vegetable oil in a deep-sided skillet or wok to 375 degrees F (190 degrees C).

Step 4 Shake excess cornstarch from the beef slices, and drop them in to the hot oil, a few at the same time. Stir briefly, and fry before edges become crisp and begin to brown, about 2 minutes. Take away the beef from the oil with a big slotted spoon, and invite to drain in some recoverable format towels to eliminate excess oil.

Step 5 Pour the oil out of your skillet or wok, and return the pan to medium heat. Return the beef slices to the pan, stir briefly, and pour in the reserved sauce. Stir a few times to mix, and add the green onions. Bring the mixture to a boil, and cook before onions have softened and turned bright green, about 2 minutes.

45. Mongolian Beef I Recipe

Ingredients

1 teaspoon sesame seeds
1 tablespoon soy sauce
1 tablespoon cornstarch
2 cloves garlic, minced
1 pound beef round steak, cut into thin strips
3/4 cup water
2 tablespoons soy sauce
2 1/2 teaspoons cornstarch
1/2 teaspoon white sugar
1 teaspoon red pepper flakes
2 tablespoons vegetable oil, divided
2 medium (blank)s carrots, thinly sliced
1 bunch green onions, cut into 2 inch pieces

Directions

Step one 1 In a dry skillet over medium heat, toast sesame seeds for 1 to2 minutes, or before seeds begin to carefully turn golden brown; set aside.

Step two 2 In a medium bowl, mix together 1 tablespoon soy sauce, 1 tablespoon cornstarch, and minced garlic. Stir in beef strips. Let are a symbol of at least 10 minutes.

Step 3 3 In another normal size bowl, mix together water, 2 tablespoons soy sauce, 2 1/2 teaspoons cornstarch, sugar, sesame seeds, and red pepper flakes; reserve.

Step 4 Heat 1 tablespoon of oil in a wok or skillet over high temperature. Cook and stir beef in hot oil for 1 minute; remove, and reserve. Heat remaining tablespoon of oil in the same pan. Saute carrots and white part of green onions for 2 minutes. Stir in green elements of the green onion, and saute for 1 minute. Stir in sesame seed mixture and beef. Cook and stir until sauce boils and thickens.

46. Mongolian Beef II

Ingredients

2 pounds boneless sirloin tip roast
1/2 cup soy sauce
2 tablespoons dry sherry
2 teaspoons sesame oil
3 tablespoons cornstarch
2 tablespoons brown sugar
2 teaspoons crushed red pepper
5 peppers whole dried red chile peppers
cup ? vegetable oil, divided
4 bunches green onions, cut into 2 inch pieces

Directions

Step one 1 Partially freeze the roast for easier slicing. Cut the roast into 3x1/2 inch strips, and reserve.

Step 2 2 In a big bowl, combine well the soy sauce, sherry, sesame oil, cornstarch, brown sugar, crushed red pepper and whole hot peppers. Place beef in the mixture and coat well. Cover and refrigerate for 20 to thirty minutes.

Step three 3 Heat 2 tablespoons of the oil in a big skillet or wok over medium high temperature. Place green onions in the hot oil. Cover, reduce heat to low and cook 6 minutes, or until tender. Remove green onions and reserve.

Step 4 In the same skillet or wok, heat remaining 1/4 cup of oil over medium high temperature. Add beef mixture and saute for five minutes, or before beef is thoroughly cooked. Return green onions to the pan and saute for 30 seconds more, or until heated through.

47. Moo Goo Gai Pan Recipe

Ingredients

1 tablespoon vegetable oil
1 cup sliced fresh mushrooms
2 cups chopped broccoli florets
1 (8-ounce) can sliced bamboo shoots, drained
1 (8-ounce) can sliced water chestnuts, drained
1 (15-ounce) can whole straw mushrooms, drained
1 tablespoon vegetable oil
2 cloves garlic, minced
1 pound skinless, boneless chicken breasts, cut into strips
1 tablespoon cornstarch
1 tablespoon white sugar
1 tablespoon soy sauce
1 tablespoon oyster sauces
1 tablespoon rice wine
1/4 cup chicken broth

Directions

Step one 1 Heat 1 tablespoon of vegetable oil in a wok or large skillet over high temperature until it begins to smoke. Stir in the new mushrooms, broccoli, bamboo shoots, water chestnuts, and straw mushrooms. Cook and stir until all of the vegetables are hot, and the broccoli is tender, about five minutes. Remove from the wok, and reserve. Wipe out the wok.

Step 2 2 Heat the rest of the tablespoon of vegetable in the wok until it begins to smoke. Stir in the garlic, and cook for a couple seconds until it turns golden-brown. Add the chicken, and cook before chicken has lightly browned on the edges, and is no more pink in the guts, about five minutes. Stir together the cornstarch, sugar, soy sauce, oyster sauce, rice wine, and chicken broth in a little bowl. Pour over the chicken, and bring to a boil, stirring constantly. Boil for approximately 30 seconds before sauce thickens and is no more cloudy. Return the vegetables to the wok, and toss with the sauce.

48. Orange Peel Beef Recipe

Ingredients

1 1/2 pounds beef top sirloin, thinly sliced
1 tablespoon low-sodium soy sauce
1 tablespoon cornstarch
1 teaspoon dark sesame oil
1/2 teaspoon baking soda
1 tablespoon low-sodium soy sauce
2 tablespoons frozen orange juice concentrate, thawed
1 tablespoon rice vinegar
1 teaspoon dark sesame oil
1 tablespoon brown sugar
1 teaspoon cornstarch
1 tablespoon peanut oil
3 cloves garlic, minced
1 tablespoon minced fresh ginger root
1 tablespoon finely shredded orange zest
1/4 teaspoon red pepper flakes

Directions

Step one 1 Combine the beef, 1 tablespoon of soy sauce, 1 tablespoon cornstarch, 1 teaspoon sesame oil, and baking soda in a bowl and mix thoroughly. Cover and refrigerate 1 to 3 hours.

Step two 2 Heat peanut oil in a wok or large, nonstick skillet over high temperature. Stir in garlic, ginger, orange zest, and red pepper flakes, and cook before garlic begins to brown, 20 to 30 seconds. Add the beef; cook and stir before beef begins to brown and crisp, about five minutes. Whisk together 1 tablespoon soy sauce, orange juice concentrate, rice vinegar, 1 teaspoon sesame oil, brown sugar, and 1 teaspoon cornstarch in a little bowl. Stir in to the beef, and cook before sauce has thickened and turned clear, about 30 seconds.

49. Peking Duck Recipe

Ingredients

1 (4 pound) whole duck, dressed
1/2 teaspoon ground cinnamon
1/2 teaspoon ground ginger
1/4 teaspoon ground nutmeg
1/4 teaspoon ground white peppers
teaspoon ? ground cloves
3 tablespoons soy sauce
1 tablespoon honey
1 orange, sliced in rounds
1 tablespoon chopped fresh parsley, for garnish
5 medium (4-1/8" long)s green onions
1/2 cup plums jam
1 1/2 teaspoons sugar
1 1/2 teaspoons distilled white vinegar
1/4 cup finely chopped chutney

Directions

Step one 1 Rinse the duck inside and out, and pat dry. Take off tail and discard. In a little bowl, mix together the cinnamon, ginger, nutmeg, white pepper and cloves. Sprinkle one teaspoon of the mixture in to the cavity of the duck. Stir one tablespoon of the soy sauce in to the remaining spice mixture and rub evenly over the complete beyond the bird. Cut among the green onions in two and tuck in the cavity. Cover and refrigerate the bird for at least 2 hours, or overnight.

Step two 2 Place duck breast side through to a rack in a big enough wok or pot and steam for one hour adding a bit more water, if necessary, since it evaporates. Lift duck with two large spoons, and drain juices and green onion.

Step three 3 Preheat the oven to 375 degrees F (190 degrees C). Place duck breast side up in a roasting pan and prick skin around using a fork.

Step 4 Roast for thirty minutes in the preheated oven. As the duck is roasting, mix together the rest of the 2 tablespoons of soy sauce and honey. After thirty minutes, brush the honey mixture onto the duck and return it to the oven. Turn heat up to 500 degrees F (260 degrees C). Roast for five minutes, or before skin is richly browned. Don't allow the skin to char.

Step 5 Prepare the duck sauce by mixing the plum jam with the sugar, vinegar and chutney in a little serving bowl. Chop remaining green onions and place them right into a separate bowl. Place whole duck onto a serving platter and garnish with orange slices and fresh parsley. Use plum sauce and onions for dipping.

50. Peking Pork Chops Recipe

Ingredients

6 ounces pork chops raw chop with refuse 113 g; (blank) 4 thick cut pork chops (1 inch)
1/4 cup brown sugar brown sugar
1 teaspoon ginger ground ginger
1/2 cup soy sauce soy sauce
1/4 cup ketchup ketchup
1 clove garlic garlic crushed
pepper salt and pepper to taste

Directions

Step 1 1 Trim extra fat from pork chops and place in slow cooker. Mix brown sugar, ginger, soy sauce, ketchup, garlic, salt and pepper in normal size bowl and pour over meat. Cover, turn to low and cook four to six 6 hours, or until tender. Season with salt and pepper, if needed.

51. Potstickers (Chinese Dumplings)

Ingredients

1 pound raw shrimp, peeled and deveined
4 pounds ground beef
1 tablespoon minced fresh ginger root
1 shallot, minced
1 bunch green onions, chopped
3 leaves napa cabbage, chopped
2 tablespoons soy sauce
1 teaspoon asian (toasted) sesame oil
1 pinch salt and white pepper to taste
1 pinch white sugar
1 (10-ounce) package round gyoza/potsticker wrappers
3 tablespoons vegetable oil
1/4 cup water

Directions

Step one 1 Place the shrimp in the task plate of a food processor, and process before shrimp are finely ground. Reserve in a large bowl. Employed in batches, process the bottom beef to an excellent grind, and reserve with the shrimp. Combine the shrimp and ground beef with ginger, shallot, green onions, napa cabbage, soy sauce, sesame oil, salt and pepper, and white sugar, and mix the Ingredients until thoroughly combined.

Step two 2 To fill the pot stickers, place a wrapper on a work surface before you, and place a scant teaspoon of completing the guts. With a wet finger, dampen the edges of the wrapper. Fold the dough right into a half-moon shape, enclosing the filling, and press and seal to eliminate extra air and tightly seal the edges together. It's nice to fold several small pleats in the very best half of the wrapper for a normal look before you seal in the filling. Refrigerate the filled wrappers on a parchment-lined baking sheet when you finish filling and sealing the pot stickers.

Step three 3 Heat the oil in a big nonstick skillet with a lid over medium heat. Place pot stickers in to the hot oil, flat sides down, without crowding, and let fry before bottoms are golden brown, one to two 2 minutes. Turn the dumplings over, and pour the water over them. Cover the pan with a lid and allow dumplings steam before water has nearly evaporated and the dumplings have begun to fry in oil again, 5 to 7 minutes. Uncover the skillet, and allow pot stickers cook until all of the water is evaporated and the wrapper has shrunk down tightly onto the filling, another 2-3 3 minutes.

52. Restaurant Style Beef and Broccoli

Ingredients

1/3 cup dry sherry
1/3 cup oyster sauces
2 teaspoons asian (toasted) sesame oil
1 teaspoon soy sauce
1 teaspoon white sugar
1 teaspoon cornstarch
1 1/2 pounds beef sirloin steak, trimmed and cut into 1/8-inch-thick slices
3 tablespoons vegetable oil, plus more if needed
1 thin slice fresh ginger root
1 clove garlic, minced
1 pound broccoli, cut into florets
1 (16-ounce) can sliced mushrooms, drained
8 ounces snow peas

Directions

Step one 1 Whisk sherry, oyster sauce, sesame oil, soy sauce, sugar, and cornstarch together in a bowl until sugar dissolves.

Step two 2 Arrange steak slices in a shallow bowl, pour the oyster sauce mixture over the meat, stir to coat, and refrigerate at least thirty minutes.

Step three 3 Heat vegetable oil in a wok or large skillet over medium-high heat. Cook and stir ginger and garlic in hot oil until fragrant about 1 minute. Remove and discard the ginger and garlic. Stir broccoli, mushrooms, and snow peas together in the skillet; cook and stir in the hot oil before broccoli is bright green and almost tender, 5 to 7 minutes. Take away the vegetable mixture to a bowl.

Step 4 Pour beef slices with the marinade in to the skillet; cook and stir before sauce forms a glaze on the beef and the meat is no more pink, about five minutes. Return the cooked vegetables to the wok; cook and stir before broccoli is heated through, about three minutes.

53. Shrimp with Lobster Sauce

Ingredients

1 1/2 teaspoons cornstarch
2 teaspoons cooking sherry
1 pound medium shrimp - peeled and deveined
1/4 cup vegetable oil
2 tablespoons garlic, minced
1/4 pound ground pork
1 cup water
2 tablespoons soy sauce
1/4 teaspoon sugar
1/2 teaspoon salt
1 1/2 tablespoons cornstarch
1/4 cup cold water
1 egg, beaten

Directions

Step one 1 In a medium bowl, dissolve 1 1/2 teaspoons of cornstarch in the sherry. Add shrimp to the bowl, and toss to coat.

Step two 2 Heat oil in a wok or large skillet over medium-high heat. Add shrimp, and fry until pink, three to five five minutes. Remove shrimp to a plate with a slotted spoon, leaving as much oil in the pan as possible. Add garlic to the hot oil, and fry for a couple seconds, then add the bottom pork. Cook, stirring constantly until pork is no more pink.

Step three 3 Combine 1 cup water, soy sauce, sugar and salt; stir in to the wok with the pork. Bring to a boil, cover, reduce heat to medium, and simmer for approximately 2 minutes. Mix together the rest of the 1 1 /2 tablespoons of cornstarch and 1/4 cup cool water. Pour in to the pan with the pork, and in addition return shrimp to the pan. Go back to a simmer, and quickly stir while drizzling in the beaten egg. Serve hot over rice.

54. Slow Cooker Mongolian Beef

Ingredients

1 pound flank steak, cut into bite-size pieces
1/4 cup cornstarch
2 teaspoons olive oil
1 onion, thinly sliced
1 tablespoon minced garlic
3 large green onions, sliced diagonally into 1/2 inch pieces
1/2 cup soy sauce
1/2 cup water
1/2 cup brown sugar
1/2 teaspoon minced fresh ginger root
1/2 cup hoisin sauce

Directions

Step one 1 Place flank steak and cornstarch right into a resealable plastic bag. Shake the bag to evenly coat the flank steak with the cornstarch. Allow to steak rest for ten minutes.

Step 2 2 Heat essential olive oil in a big skillet over medium-high heat. Cook and stir steak until evenly browned, 2 to 4 minutes. Place onion, garlic, flank steak, green onions, soy sauce, water, brown sugar, ginger, and hoisin sauce in a slow cooker. Cook on Low setting for approximately 4 hours.

55. Spicy Beef Filet in Oyster Sauce

Ingredients

1 1/2 teaspoons vegetable oil
1 1/2 teaspoons oyster sauces
3/4 teaspoon cornstarch
1 pound beef tenderloin, cut into 1/4 inch strips
1 1/2 teaspoons water
1 1/2 teaspoons cornstarch
3 tablespoons oyster sauces
1 1/2 teaspoons sugar
1 1/2 teaspoons black pepper
1 1/2 tablespoons vegetable oil
3/4 onion, thinly sliced

Directions

Step one 1 Stir together 1 teaspoon vegetable oil, 1 teaspoon oyster sauce, and 1/2 teaspoon cornstarch in a bowl. Add beef and toss to coat. Marinate in the refrigerator 30 to 45 minutes. Remove from the refrigerator ten minutes before cooking.

Step two 2 Stir together water, 1 teaspoon cornstarch, 2 tablespoons oyster sauce, and pepper in a little bowl; reserve. Heat 1 tablespoon vegetable oil in a big skillet over high temperature. Stir in onion, and cook until it beings to brown on the edges, about 1 minute. Add the beef, and continue cooking and stirring before beef is merely slightly pink, about five minutes. Pour in the sauce; cook and stir before sauce has thickened and turned translucent, about 1 minute more.

56. Spicy Crispy Beef Recipe

Ingredients

1/4 cup cornstarch
1/4 tablespoon salt
black pepper
12 ounces flank steak, thinly sliced
1 quart oils for frying
4 tablespoons soy sauce
1 tablespoon rice vinegar
1/2 tablespoon rice wine
1 1/2 tablespoons honey
7 tablespoons granulated sugar
1/2 tablespoon chile paste
1/4 cup water
3 tablespoons chopped fresh ginger root
1 tablespoon vegetable oil
2 cloves garlic, chopped
1/4 cup sliced onions
1/4 cup diced red bell pepper

Directions

Step one 1 Heat oil in deep-fryer to 375 degrees F (190 degrees C).

Step two 2 Meanwhile, in a mixing bowl, combine cornstarch, salt and pepper together. Mix thoroughly. Toss the steak slices in the cornstarch mixture and coat well.

Step three 3 Deep fry the coated steak slices until golden brown. Check to ensure they are cooked through. Remove from oil, and reserve.

Step 4 In another mixing bowl, combine the soy sauce, rice vinegar, rice wine and honey. Add sugar, chili paste, water, and ginger. Mix well and reserve.

Step 5 Heat a wok or deep frying pan over medium high temperature. Add 1 tablespoon of oil, and quickly saute the onion, garlic and red pepper for 30 seconds. Add the sauce mixture, and cook another 30 seconds. Finally, add the strips of fried steak and toss to heat through and coat with sauce.

57. Spicy Orange Zest Beef

Ingredients

1 pound beef tenderloin, cut into 1/2 inch strips
1/4 cup orange juice
1/4 cup seasoned rice vinegar
2 tablespoons soy sauce
1 tablespoon hot chile paste (such as sambal oelek)
1 tablespoon brown sugar, or to taste
2 cloves garlic, minced
1/4 cup water
1 teaspoon cornstarch
cooking spray
2 tablespoons grated orange zest
1 bunch green onions, sliced - white parts and tops separated
salt and freshly ground black pepper to taste

Directions

Combine beef, orange juice, rice vinegar, soy sauce, hot chili paste, brown sugar, and garlic in a big bowl. Cover and refrigerate for one to two 2 hours.

Strain beef in a colander set over a big bowl, allowing beef to drain thoroughly, about five minutes. Reserve marinade.

Stir water and cornstarch in to the plate of marinade. Whisk until cornstarch is dissolved, reserve.

Spray skillet with cooking spray and place over high temperature. Cook beef for 1 minute without stirring; cook and stir for yet another minute.

Stir in light elements of green onion and orange zest; cook for 30 seconds.

Stir in marinade and green onion tops; cook and stir until beef is no more pink inside and sauce is reduced and thick, about 2-3 3 minutes.

Season with salt and black pepper to taste.

58. Steamed Fish with Ginger

Ingredients

1 pound halibut fillet
1 teaspoon coarse sea salt or kosher salt
1 tablespoon minced fresh ginger
3 tablespoons thinly sliced green onions
1 tablespoon dark soy sauce
1 tablespoon light soy sauce
1 tablespoon peanut oil
2 teaspoons toasted sesame oil
1/4 cup lightly packed fresh cilantro sprigs

Directions

Step one 1 Pat halibut dry with paper towels. Rub both sides of fillet with salt. Scatter the ginger outrageous of the fish and place onto a heatproof ceramic dish.

Step 2 2 Place right into a bamboo steamer set over several inches of gently boiling water, and cover. Gently steam for 10 to 12 minutes.

Step three 3 Pour accumulated water out from the dish and sprinkle the fillet with green onion. Drizzle both soy sauces over the top of fish.

Step 4 Heat peanut and sesame oils in a little skillet over medium-high heat until linked with emotions . smoke. When the oil is hot, carefully pour along with the halibut fillet. The hot oil may cause the green onions and water along with the fish to pop and spatter around; be cautious. Garnish with cilantro sprigs and serve immediately.

59. Stir-Fried Chicken With Pineapple and Peppers

Ingredients

2 1/2 tablespoons reduced-salt soy sauce
1 1/2 tablespoons white wine vinegar
1 1/2 tablespoons mirin (sweetened asian wine)
2/3 teaspoon grated ginger root
1 1/3 garlic clove (blank)s crushed garlic cloves
2 teaspoons cornstarch
1 1/2 tablespoons oil, preferably sesame oil
2/3 pound boneless, skinless chicken breasts, cut in 1-inch pieces
4 large green onions, cut in 1-inch pieces
1 1/3 cups fresh or frozen pepper strips
2/3 (20-ounce) can chunk pineapple in juice
2 1/2 tablespoons sliced almonds

Directions

Step one 1 Combine first six Ingredients; stir well.

Step two 2 Heat oil in a big skillet and stir-fry chicken until brown and done, about five minutes. Remove. Add green onions, peppers and pineapple to the skillet; heat through. Pour in sauce and stir until thickened. Return chicken to skillet; heat through. Serve with brown rice; top with optional almonds.

60. Stir-Fry Pork with Ginger

Ingredients

2 tablespoons vegetable oil
1/2 inch piece fresh ginger root, thinly sliced
1/4 pound thinly sliced lean pork
1 teaspoon soy sauce
1/2 teaspoon dark soy sauce
1/2 teaspoon salt
1/3 teaspoon sugar
1 teaspoon sesame oil
1 green onion, chopped
1 tablespoon chinese rice wine

Directions

Step one 1 Heat oil in a big skillet or wok over medium-high heat. Fry ginger in hot oil until fragrant, then add pork, soy sauce, dark soy sauce, salt, and sugar. Cook, stirring occasionally, for ten minutes.

Step two 2 Stir in the sesame oil, green onion, and rice wine. Simmer before pork is tender.

61. Super-Spicy Mongolian Beef

Ingredients

1/4 cup soy sauce
1 tablespoon hoisin sauce
1 tablespoon sesame oil
2 teaspoons white sugar
1 tablespoon minced garlic
1 tablespoon red pepper flakes
1 pound beef flank steak, thinly sliced
1 tablespoon peanut oil
2 large green onions, thinly sliced

Directions

Step one 1 Whisk together soy sauce, hoisin sauce, sesame oil, sugar, garlic, and red pepper flakes in a bowl. Toss beef with marinade, cover, and refrigerate one hour to overnight.

Step two 2 Heat peanut oil in a wok or large, nonstick skillet over high temperature. Add the green onions, and cook for 5 to 10 seconds before stirring in the beef.

Cook and stir before beef is no more pink and is starting to brown, about 5 minutes.

62. Super-Spicy Mongolian Beef Recipe

Ingredients

1/4 cup soy sauce
1 tablespoon hoisin sauce
1 tablespoon sesame oil
2 teaspoons white sugar
1 tablespoon minced garlic
1 tablespoon red pepper flakes
1 pound beef flank steak, thinly sliced
1 tablespoon peanut oil
2 large green onions, thinly sliced

Directions

Step one 1 Whisk together soy sauce, hoisin sauce, sesame oil, sugar, garlic, and red pepper flakes in a bowl. Toss beef with marinade, cover, and refrigerate one hour to overnight.

Step two 2 Heat peanut oil in a wok or large, nonstick skillet over high temperature. Add the green onions, and cook for 5 to 10 seconds before stirring in the beef. Cook and stir before beef is no more pink and is starting to brown, about 5 minutes.

63. Sweet and Sour Chicken I

Ingredients

3/4 (8-ounce) can pineapple chunks, drained (juice reserved)
3 tablespoons cornstarch
1 1/3 cups water, divided
1/2 cup white sugar
6 tablespoons distilled white vinegar
1 1/2 drops orange food colors
6 whole breast (blank)s skinless, boneless chicken breasts halves - cut into 1 inch cubes
1 2/3 cups self-rising flour
1 1/2 tablespoons vegetable oil
1 1/2 tablespoons cornstarch
3/8 teaspoon salt
3/16 teaspoon ground white peppers
3/4 egg
1 cup water
3 cups vegetable oil for frying
1 1/2 medium (blank)s green bell pepper, cut into 1 inch pieces

Directions

Step one 1 In a saucepan, combine 1 1/2 cups water, sugar, vinegar, reserved pineapple juice, and orange food coloring. Heat to boiling. Switch off heat. Combine 1/4 cup cornstarch and 1/4 cup water; slowly stir into saucepan. Continue stirring until mixture thickens.

Step two 2 Combine flour, 2 tablespoons oil, 2 tablespoons cornstarch, salt, white pepper, and egg. Add 1 1/2 cups water gradually to generate a thick batter. Stir to blend thoroughly. Add chicken pieces, and stir until chicken is well coated.

Step three 3 Heat oil in skillet or wok to 360 degrees F (180 degrees C). Fry chicken pieces in hot oil ten minutes, or until golden. Remove chicken, and drain in some recoverable format towels.

Step 4 4 When prepared to serve, layer green peppers, pineapple chunks, and cooked chicken pieces on a platter. Pour hot sweet and sour sauce over top.

64. Sweet and Sour Pork III

Ingredients

1 pound pork butt, cut into 1 inch cubes
1 teaspoon salt
1/4 teaspoon white sugar
1 teaspoon soy sauce
1 egg white
2 medium (4-1/8" long)s green onions, chopped
1 quart vegetable oil for frying
1/2 cup cornstarch
1 tablespoon vegetable oil
3 stalks celery, cut into 1/2 inch pieces
1 medium green bell pepper, cut into 1 inch pieces
1 medium onion, cut into wedges
1 pinch white sugar to taste
1 pinch salt to taste
1 cup water
1/4 teaspoon salt
3/4 cup white sugar
1/3 cup apple cider vinegar
1/4 cup ketchup
1/2 teaspoon soy sauce

1 (8-ounce) can pineapple chunks, undrained
2 tablespoons cornstarch
1/4 cup water

Directions

Step one 1 Place cubed pork in a medium bowl, and season with 1 teaspoon salt, 1/4 teaspoon sugar, and 1 teaspoon soy sauce. Mix in the egg white and green onions. Cover, and place in the refrigerator at least one hour.

Step two 2 Heat 1 quart oil to 365 degrees F (185 degrees C) in a big, heavy saucepan or deep fryer.

Step three 3 Coat the pork with 1/2 cup cornstarch, and fry in the heated oil about ten minutes, until evenly browned. Drain in some recoverable format towels.

Step 4 Heat 1 tablespoon oil in a wok over medium heat. Stir in the celery, green bell pepper, and onion, and cook until tender. Season with salt and sugar. Remove from heat, and reserve.

Step 5 In a big saucepan, mix 1 cup water, 1/4 teaspoon salt, 3/4 cup sugar, apple cider vinegar, ketchup, and 1/2 teaspoon soy sauce. Bring to a boil, and stir in the cooked pork, celery mixture, and the pineapple chunks with juice. Go back to boil, and mix in 2 tablespoons cornstarch and 1/4 cup water to thicken. Cook until well blended.

65. Sweet and Sour Pork Tenderloin Recipe

Ingredients

1 (1 1/4 pound) pork tenderloin, trimmed of silver skin
salt and ground black pepper
1/3 cup ketchup
1/3 cup seasoned rice vinegar
1 (8-ounce) can pineapple chunks, drained with juice reserved
2 tablespoons brown sugar
4 cloves garlic, minced
2 teaspoons hot chili sauce (such as sriracha®)
1 teaspoon soy sauce
1 pinch red pepper flakes
1 tablespoon vegetable oil
1 teaspoon butter
1/4 cup chopped green onions (white part only)
2 tablespoons chopped green onions tops

Directions

Cut tenderloin into 4 pieces. Arrange in one layer between two sheets of plastic wrap and pound with a meat mallet until each is approximately 1-inch thick. Generously season with salt and black pepper.

Whisk ketchup, rice vinegar, reserved pineapple juice, brown sugar, garlic, hot chili sauce, soy sauce, and red pepper flakes in a bowl. Reserve.

Heat vegetable oil in a skillet over high temperature. Place pork in pan; reduce heat to medium. Cook until browned on both sides and cooked through, 5 to 6 minutes per side. Transfer to a plate.

Return skillet to medium heat. Stir butter into hot pan. When butter melts and starts to brown, stir in pineapple chunks. Cook, stirring, until pineapple is golden brown, three to four 4 minutes.

Stir in ketchup mixture and 1/4 cup green onion (white parts). Reduce heat to low and simmer until garlic and onion have softened, five minutes.

Return pork to skillet; cook, stirring, until pork is heated through. Garnish with 2 tablespoons green onion tops.

66. Szechuan Beef Recipe

Ingredients

1 pound sirloin steak, cut into bite size strips
1 tablespoon soy sauce
2 teaspoons cornstarch
1/4 teaspoon crushed red pepper
1 clove garlic, minced
2 tablespoons vegetable oil
3 cups fresh broccoli florets
2 small onions, cut into wedges
1 (8-ounce) can water chestnuts, drained
1/4 cup chicken broth
1/2 cup peanuts

Directions

Toss beef with soy sauce, cornstarch, crushed red pepper and garlic in non-metal bowl. Cover and refrigerate 20 minutes.

Heat oil in wok or large skillet over high temperature. Stir fry beef until no more pink, five minutes. Stir in broccoli, onions and water chestnuts; cook 2 minutes. Pour in broth, and bring to a boil. Stir in peanuts, cook about a minute more, and serve.

67. Szechuan Spicy Eggplant

Ingredients

1 (1 1/2 pound) eggplant
4 tablespoons soy sauce
1/4 cup chicken stock
1 teaspoon chili sauce
1 teaspoon white sugar
1/2 teaspoon ground black pepper
2 tablespoons oyster sauces
1 tablespoon cornstarch
4 tablespoons water
2 cloves garlic, minced
4 large green onions, finely chopped
1 tablespoon chopped fresh ginger root
1/4 pound fresh shrimp - peeled, deveined, and diced
1/3 pound lean ground beef
1 tablespoon sesame oil
4 cups hot cooked rice

Directions

Step 1 1 Take away the eggplant stem and cut into 1-inch cubes. In a medium bowl, combine the soy sauce, chicken stock, chili sauce, sugar, ground black pepper and oyster sauce. Stir together well and reserve. In a separate normal size bowl, combine the cornstarch and water, and reserve.

Step 2 2 Coat a big, deep pan with cooking spray over high temperature and allow a couple of minutes for it to get scorching. Saute the garlic, half of the green onions, ginger and dried shrimp, if using (see Cook's Note) for three to five five minutes, stirring constantly, until linked with emotions . brown. Stir in the bottom beef or pork and cook for 3 more minutes, again stirring constantly, until browned.

Step three 3 Pour the eggplant in to the pan and stir altogether. Pour the reserved soy sauce mixture over-all, cover the pan, reduce heat to medium low and let simmer for a quarter-hour, stirring occasionally. If you are using fresh shrimp, add it over the last short while of cooking. Stir in the reserved cornstarch mixture and let heat until thickened. Finally, stir in all of those other green onions and the sesame oil.

Step 4 Serve over hot rice.

68. Szechwan Shrimp Recipe

Ingredients

4 tablespoons water
2 tablespoons ketchup
1 tablespoon soy sauce
2 teaspoons cornstarch
1 teaspoon honey
1/2 teaspoon crushed red pepper
1/4 teaspoon ground ginger
1 tablespoon vegetable oil
1/4 cup sliced green onions
4 cloves garlic, minced
12 ounces cooked shrimp, tails removed

Directions

In a bowl, stir together water, ketchup, soy sauce, cornstarch, honey, crushed red pepper, and ground ginger. Reserve.

Heat oil in a big skillet over medium-high heat. Stir in green onions and garlic; cook 30 seconds. Stir in shrimp, and toss to coat with oil. Stir in sauce. Cook and stir until sauce is bubbly and thickened.

69. Ten Minute Szechuan Chicken Recipe

Ingredients

4 breast half, bone and skin removed (blank)s boneless skinless chicken breasts, cut into cubes
3 tablespoons cornstarch
1 tablespoon vegetable oil
4 cloves garlic, minced
5 tablespoons low-sodium soy sauce
1 1/2 tablespoons white wine vinegar
1/4 cup water
1 teaspoon white sugar
3 medium (4-1/8" long)s green onions, sliced diagonally into 1/2 inch pieces
teaspoon ? cayenne pepper, or to taste

Directions

Step one Place the chicken and cornstarch right into a bag or bowl, and toss to coat. Heat oil in a wok or large skillet over medium-high heat. Fry the chicken pieces and garlic, stirring constantly until lightly browned. Stir in the soy sauce, vinegar, sugar and water. Cover, and cook before chicken pieces are no more pink inside, three to five 5 minutes.

Step two Stir in the green onion, and cayenne pepper, cook uncovered for approximately 2 more minutes. Serve over white rice.

70. Tsao's Chicken II

Ingredients

4 cups vegetable oil for frying
1 egg
1 1/2 pounds boneless, skinless chicken thighs, cut into 1/2 inch cubes
1 teaspoon salt
1 teaspoon white sugar
1 pinch white peppers
1 cup cornstarch
2 tablespoons vegetable oil
3 tablespoons chopped green onions
1 clove garlic, minced
6 peppers dried whole red chilies
1 strip orange zest
1/2 cup white sugar
1/4 teaspoon ground ginger
3 tablespoons chicken broth
1 tablespoon rice vinegar
1/4 cup soy sauce
2 teaspoons sesame oil
2 tablespoons peanut oil
2 teaspoons cornstarch
1/4 cup water

Directions

Step one 1 Heat 4 cups vegetable oil in a deep-fryer or large saucepan to 375 degrees F (190 degrees C).

Step two 2 Beat the egg in a mixing bowl. Add the chicken cubes; sprinkle with salt, 1 teaspoon sugar, and white pepper; mix well. Mix in 1 cup of cornstarch a bit at a time before chicken cubes are well coated.

Step three 3 In batches, carefully drop the chicken cubes in to the hot oil one at a time, cooking until they turns golden brown and commence to float, about three minutes. Remove the chicken and invite to cool as you fry another batch. Once all the chicken has been fried, refry the chicken, you start with the batch that was cooked first. Cook before chicken turns deep golden brown, about 2 minutes more. Drain on a paper towel-lined plate.

Step 4 Heat 2 tablespoons vegetable oil in a wok or large skillet over high temperature. Stir in the green onion, garlic, whole chiles, and orange zest. Cook and stir just a few minutes before garlic has turned golden and the chiles brighten. Add 1/2 cup sugar, the ginger, chicken broth, vinegar, soy sauce, sesame oil, and peanut oil; bring to a boil and cook for three minutes.

Step 5 Dissolve 2 teaspoons of cornstarch in to the water, and stir in to the boiling sauce. Go back to a boil and cook before sauce thickens and is no more cloudy from the cornstarch, about 1 minute. Stir the chicken in to the boiling sauce. Reduce heat to low and cook for some minutes before chicken absorbs a few of the sauce.

Pepper Steak With Mushrooms

Ingredients
6 tablespoons reduced-sodium soy sauce, divided
1/8 teaspoon pepper
1 pound beef top sirloin steak, cut into thin strips
1 tablespoon cornstarch
1/2 cup reduced-sodium beef broth
1 garlic clove, minced
1/2 teaspoon minced fresh gingerroot
3 teaspoons canola oil, divided
1 cup julienned sweet red pepper
1 cup julienned green pepper
2 cups sliced fresh mushrooms
2 medium tomatoes, cut into wedges
6 green onions, sliced
Hot cooked rice, optional

Directions
In a shallow bowl, combine 3 tablespoons soy sauce and pepper; add beef. Turn to coat; cover and refrigerate 30-60 minutes. In a small bowl, combine the cornstarch, broth and remaining soy sauce until smooth; set aside.

Drain beef, discarding marinade. In a large nonstick skillet or wok, stir-fry the garlic and ginger in 2 teaspoons oil for 1 minute. Add the beef; stir-fry 4-6 minutes or until no longer pink. Remove beef and keep warm.

Stir-fry the peppers in remaining oil for 1 minute. Add mushrooms; stir-fry 2 minutes longer or until peppers are crisp-tender. Stir broth mixture and add to vegetable mixture. Bring to a boil; cook and stir for 2 minutes or until thickened.

Return beef to pan; add tomatoes and onions. Cook for 2 minutes or until heated through. Serve over rice if desired.

Sesame Beef Stir fry

Ingredients
½ pound beef (sirloin is recommended)
1 ½ tablespoons sesame seeds
1 large broccoli floret
½ sweet yellow bell pepper
½ cup beef stock
2 tablespoons soy sauce
1 tablespoon ginger
1 large garlic clove
1 teaspoon cornstarch
¼ teaspoon red hot chili peppers (crushed)
3 tablespoons vegetable oil

Directions
Combine beef strips with 1½ tablespoons sesame seeds in small bowl. Toss to coat well.

Cut florets off broccoli stalk. Peel stalk and thinly slice. Combine broccoli florets and stalk with yellow pepper in medium bowl.

Stir broth, soy sauce, ginger, garlic, cornstarch, and crushed red pepper in small bowl until cornstarch dissolves.

Heat 1½ tablespoons oil in wok or heavy large skillet over high heat. Add beef and stir-fry until brown, for 2 minutes. Using slotted spoon, transfer beef to plate.

Heat remaining 1½ tablespoons oil in wok.

Add broccoli, peppers and stir-fry for one minute then cover wok for 2 minutes. Add remaining ingredients, stir-fry for one minute. Add beef and liquid from plate.

Simmer until sauce thickens, stirring occasionally, for 1 minute. Transfer beef mixture to plate. Sprinkle with toasted sesame seeds and serve with rice.

Beef And Snow Pea Stir-Fry

Ingredients
1/2 cup reduced-sodium soy sauce
1/2 cup sherry or water
2 tablespoons cornstarch
2 teaspoons sugar
2 tablespoons canola oil, divided
2 garlic cloves, minced
1-1/2 pounds beef top sirloin steak, thinly sliced
1/2 pound sliced fresh mushrooms
1 medium onion, cut into thin wedges
1/2 pound fresh snow peas
Hot cooked rice, optional

Directions
In a small bowl, whisk soy sauce, sherry, cornstarch and sugar. Transfer 1/4 cup mixture to a large bowl; stir in 1 tablespoon oil and garlic. Add beef; toss to coat. Let stand 15 minutes.

Heat a large skillet over medium-high heat. Add half of the beef mixture; stir-fry for 1-2 minutes or until no longer pink. Remove from pan; repeat with remaining beef.

In the same pan, heat remaining oil over medium-high heat until hot. Add mushrooms and onion; cook and stir until mushrooms are tender. Add snow peas; cook 2-3 minutes longer or until crisp-tender.

Stir remaining soy sauce mixture and add to pan. Bring to a boil; cook and stir 1-2 minutes or until sauce is thickened. Return beef to pan; heat through. Serve with rice if desired.

Ginger Beef

Ingredients
2 large eggs, lightly beaten
2 teaspoons olive oil
1 beef top sirloin steak (3/4 pound), thinly sliced in strips
4 tablespoons reduced-sodium soy sauce, divided
1 package broccoli coleslaw mix
1 cup frozen peas
3 garlic cloves, minced
2 cups cooked white rice
4 green onions, sliced
2 tablespoons grated fresh gingerroot

Directions
In a large nonstick skillet coated with cooking spray, cook and stir eggs over medium heat until no liquid egg remains, breaking up eggs into small pieces. Remove from pan; clean skillet if necessary.

In same skillet, heat oil over medium-high heat. Add beef; stir-fry for 1-2 minutes or until no longer pink. Add in 1 tablespoon soy sauce on beef then stir and remove from skillet.

Add coleslaw mix, peas, ginger and garlic to the pan; cook and stir until coleslaw mix is crisp-tender. Add rice and remaining soy sauce, tossing to combine rice with vegetable mixture; heat through.

Add in cooked eggs, beef and green onions, stir gently and cook for 1 minute or until heated through.

Beef with Broccoli

Ingredients
1 tablespoon cornstarch
1/2 cup reduced-sodium beef broth
1/4 cup sherry or additional beef broth
2 tablespoons reduced-sodium soy sauce
1 tablespoon brown sugar
1 garlic clove, minced
1 teaspoon minced fresh gingerroot
2 teaspoons canola oil, divided
1/2 pound beef top sirloin steak, cut into 1/4-inch-thick strips
2 cups fresh small broccoli florets
8 green onions, cut into 1-inch pieces

Directions
Mix the first 7 ingredients. In a large nonstick skillet, heat 1 teaspoon oil over medium-high heat; stir-fry beef until browned, for 1-3 minutes and remove from pan.

Stir-fry broccoli in remaining oil until crisp-tender, 3-5 minutes. Add green onions; cook just until tender, 1-2 minutes. Stir cornstarch mixture and add to pan. Bring to a boil; cook and stir until sauce is thickened, 2-3 minutes. Add beef and heat through.

Spicy Beef Stir Fry

Ingredients
1 pound beef top sirloin steak, cut into thin strips
1 tablespoon minced fresh gingerroot
3 garlic cloves, minced, divided
1/4 teaspoon pepper
3/4 teaspoon salt, divided
1 cup light coconut milk
2 tablespoons sugar
1 tablespoon Sriracha chili sauce
1/2 teaspoon grated lime zest
2 tablespoons lime juice
2 tablespoons canola oil, divided
1 large sweet red pepper, cut into thin strips
1/2 medium red onion, thinly sliced
1 jalapeno pepper, seeded and thinly sliced
4 cups fresh baby spinach
2 green onions, thinly sliced
2 tablespoons chopped fresh cilantro

Directions
In a large bowl, mix beef with ginger, 2 garlic cloves, pepper and 1/2 teaspoon salt; let stand 15 minutes. In a small bowl, whisk coconut milk, sugar, chili sauce, lime zest, lime juice and remaining salt until blended.

In a large skillet, heat 1 tablespoon oil over medium-high heat. Add beef and stir-fry until no longer pink for 2-3 minutes. Remove from pan.

Stir-fry red pepper, red onion, jalapeno and remaining garlic in remaining oil just until vegetables are crisp-tender for 2-3 minutes. Stir in coconut milk mixture; heat through.

Add spinach and beef; cook until spinach is wilted and beef is heated through, stirring occasionally. Sprinkle with green onions and cilantro.

www.ingramcontent.com/pod-product-compliance
Lightning Source LLC
Chambersburg PA
CBHW071442070526
44578CB00001B/192